1000 fabulous Knit Hats

First published in the United States of America by

Quarry Books, a member of
Quayside Publishing Group
100 Cummings Center
Suite 406-L
Beverly, Massachusetts 01915-6101
Telephone: (978) 282-9590
Fax: (978) 283-2742
www.quarrybooks.com

Visit www.Craftside.Typepad.com for a behind-the-scenes peek at our crafty world!

ISBN-13: 978-1-59253-610-8
ISBN-10: 1-59253-610-7

10 9 8 7 6 5 4 3 2 1

Design: Sandra Salamony
Cover Images: Row 1: Katie Ahlquist, Woolly Wormhead, Woolly Wormhead, Harpa Jónsdóttif, Harpa Jónsdóttir. Row 2: London Nelson. Row 3: Harpa Jónsdóttir, Woolly Wormhead, Katie Ahlquist, Erin Taylor Bell, Katie Ahlquist.

Printed in China

1000
fabulous Knit Hats

Annie Modesitt

BEVERLY MASSACHUSETTS

QUARRY BOOKS

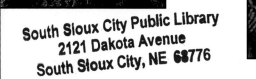

Contents

winning
Designs

section**1**

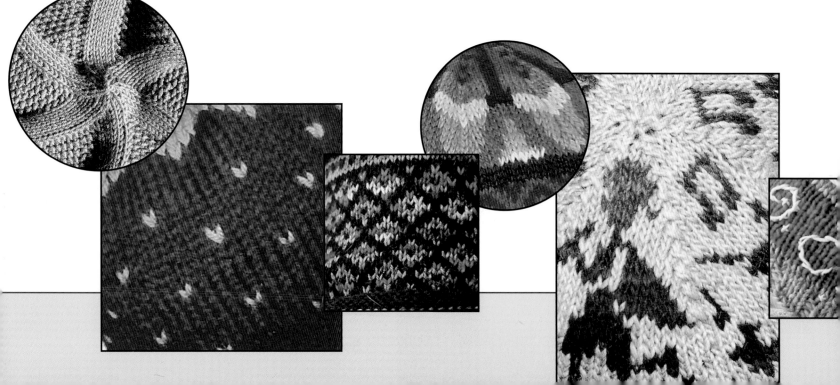

the Hats

section 2

section 3

winning Patterns

Introduction

We express ourselves in many ways; our loves, our career, our film and book choices, and—perhaps most publicly—through our clothing choices. The basic "uniform" of life, pants or skirt, shirt, and shoes, are just the starting point or our self-revelation. What really gives us away are our extracurricular garment choices. The items we may not need to wear, but want to wear because they make us feel happy.

This is how hats feel to me. Pure happiness with a touch of utility.

For most of the twentieth century, as odd as it may seem to our non–hat wearing culture, a woman would spend more on a fine piece of millinery than she might on a pair of shoes or even a dress. There are characters in history and literature who will be forever linked to their choice of hat: Lincoln's stovepipe top hat, Napoleon's bicorn, Mary Queen of Scots' French attifet (also favored by Queen Victoria), right down to Jughead's zigzag-edged cap.

A hat frames the face and accentuates the eyes, the windows of the soul. A hat can conceal a bad hair day while revealing a unique personality.

And a hat is also easy to knit or crochet.

Hats are the go-to project for a knitter or crocheter who needs something to occupy a few hours (or days) but hesitates to commit to a sock, sweater, or larger project. Quicker to work up than a scarf, easier to shape than a mitten, a hat is a perfect project. It can be as simple as a watch cap to keep the pate toasty on a chilly morning, an expression of political solidarity, or a canvas for stunning cabling and intricate lace work.

A hat can be worked from the top down or the bottom up, side to side, or even on a diagonal and folded, origami-like, into a wearable shape. Every human on the planet has probably, at one point in time, worn some semblance of a hat—even if it's just a newspaper laid on the head to keep the sun out of the eyes.

A hand-created hat contains all the beauty of the yarn, the invention of the pattern, and also something more—a piece of the soul of the person who works the stitches. With each row, with every repeat of a motif, the knitter or crocheter cannot help but wonder about the recipient of his or her hard work: Will the wearer like the hat? Grow to love it? Will it become a treasured, never-leave-the-house-without-it garment, a signature piece? Will it protect a loved one from the cold? Impart to a not-yet-known friend that she is loved as she undergoes a chemo treatment?

This exploration of hats created with yarn and two needles or one hook reflects the work of many talented crafters and represents a wide variety of hats in myriad shapes, fibers, colors, embellishments, and with multiple purposes. Some hats are for warmth, and some are for fun, but most fall somewhere in between.

After all, there's no law that says our brains can't be as well dressed as the rest of our bodies!

Annie Modesitt

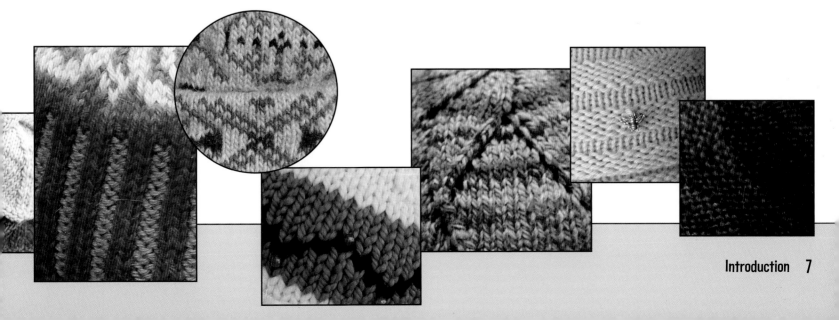

The Judging Process

𝒪𝓃𝑒 𝓉𝒽𝑜𝓊𝓈𝒶𝓃𝒹 is a big number. I think we get used to millions, billions, and even trillions being tossed around, but when you come right down to it, how many of us have SEEN 1,000 of anything in a group?

The skill—both in knitting and in photography—that was shared by the contributors in this book is astounding, and made the judging process for the top 10 hats very difficult.

Choosing the Top Ten

These hats represent some of the most beautiful hats I've seen. The decision-making process was a great joy and a great difficulty, but ultimately proved very inspiring. My goal was to create a list of 10 hats that represented a broad cross-section all the pieces in the book.

To this end, I may have selected a colorwork hat over a lace hat, or a cabled hat over a colorwork hat, not just because of the beauty of the winning hat, but also because it suited the entire list. I wanted to represent a hat from each knitting category (lace, color, gansey, etc.) in the top 10, and above all I wanted to include hats that I felt would be extremely fun to work up!

The Criteria

First and foremost, the hat had to be ABLE to be duplicated. I received some astoundingly beautiful submissions, hats whose artistry blew me away, but that were obviously one-of-a-kind pieces that couldn't be recreated using any kind of written instruction.

The pattern had to be original and the work of the person submitting the hat.

The hat had to be an enjoyable knit. I didn't want the process of creating something to keep the outside of the head warm to hurt the inside of the head by taxing the brain too severely.

The hat had to be beautiful, compelling, and inspiring.

The photograph of the hat had to be high resolution and also beautiful. It was vitally important that the top 10 hats have images that were clear and easy to read.

The Patterns

The patterns for these top 10 beautiful hats can be found in the back of the book, beginning on page 300. I'd like to thank these talented knit designers for sharing their work. Read on to learn more about our winning designers.

Spinning Designs

1st place

0001

Flowers

Designed & Contributed by Harpa Jónsdóttir
ICELAND

Harpa Jónsdóttir's contributions to the book were jaw-droppingly brilliant. As soon as I saw the way she'd worked knitting, felting, and embroidery into such delicate hats, I knew that she'd be among the top prize winners.

The acid test, though, was whether her vision could be recreated in a workable hat pattern. I'm very happy with the amount of detail, inspiration, and personality that comes through in Harpa's pattern, and I love her sense that "This is YOUR hat!"—the notion to make it your own, which shines through her work.

2nd place

0002

End of May Hat

Designed & Contributed by Mandy Powers
USA

Colorwork is one of the most satisfying ways to create a beautiful piece of knit fabric. Mandy Powers's hat summed up for me the excitement of stranding two colors to create a whole greater than the sum of the individual yarns. Her detailing at the hem and top of the hat were what pushed this into the top 10.

3rd place

0003

Is It Spring Yet?

Designed & Contributed by Constance M. Cole
CANADA

Constance M. Cole's lovely piece went a step beyond my stated criteria. Her hat was not only lovely and fun to work up, and demonstrated a bedrock knit technique (lace), but it also was in one of the most popular shapes submitted for the book—the simple beret! I knew I wanted to include a beret, and I wanted to include a lovely lace hat—who knew I'd find both of them together!?

The next 7 hats in the top 10 aren't runners-up as much as they're ambassadors from the various domains of knitting. I feel they represent a distillation of each technique, a clear vision, and—most important—a fun project!

0004

Lavender Lattice

Designed & Contributed by Mary Keenan
CANADA

This hat was chosen for the simple way a complex technique is incorporated into a lovely hat. The skill set necessary to create this hat isn't large, but the results are very impressive.

0005

Altay Hat Kureyon

Contributed by ChezPlum, Designed by Sylvie Damey
FRANCE

The only crocheted hat in the top 10, this wonderful little pointed chapeau has a construction that is quite intruiging. It's also a wonderful project for new or experienced crocheters and can use just about any yarn.

0006

Two-Toned Baby Hat
Designed & Contributed by Katie Ahlquist
USA

The structure of this hat is very intruiging: it is worked in the round, but uses two blocks of color. The technique for this involves a type of short row, and is simpler than one might expect. It is a nice touch to see the use of gray in a baby hat, too!

0007

Hat for Warm Necks

Designed & Contributed by Ellen M. Silva, TwinSet
Designs
USA

Gansey technique isn't seen as often in hats as it should be. The
use of only knits and purls to create illustrations is fun to do, and
simple enough that even a very new knitter can make a simple
gansey pattern. The structure of this hat is wonderful, too—after all,
wouldn't we all like a warm neck?

0008

Igloo

Designed & Contributed by Woolly Wormhead
UK

Perhaps the most eclectic contributor to our collection of
hats, Woolly Wormhead is becoming a household name
in knit hat circles. The unexpected shaping in this hat is
clever, funny, and at the same time practical!

0010

Cabled Tie Topper

Contributed by Tot Toppers, Designed by Kathryn L. Oates
USA

Here is a lovely example of cables, stranded colors, and texture knitting all in one adorable little hat. The fact that it's a baby hat makes the prospect of all those color changes worked in knit and purl a little less daunting, and the I-cord tip is a wonderful celebration of the finish of this hat!

0009

Pointy Striped Color

Designed & Contributed by Tori Seierstad, Torirot Design
NORWAY

The harmony of the colorwork chart for this hat made me feel it would be a perfect representation of a hat worked in the fair isle technique. The hat is featured in two colorways (see page 311), showing that the chart can be reinterpreted to work with any collection of loose ends and odd balls.

Photo by KSC Photography

- Hat Shapes
- Stitch Techniques
- Specialty: Babies & Children

the Hats

0012 | Short Row Knit Tam, Designed & Contributed by Rebecca Harmon

0011 | Multi Disco Beret, Contributed by ChezPlum, Designed by Sylvie Damey

0013 | Pagoda Hat 1, Contributed by Kristi L Knits, Designed by Kristi Founds

0015 | Malabrigo Disco Beret, Contributed by ChezPlum, Designed by Sylvie Damey

0016 | Kaleidoscope Tam, Designed & Contributed by Amy Polcyn

0014 | Traversa & 2 Merets, Contributed by Yvonne Allen, Designed by Woolly Wormhead

0017 | Adjustable Chemo Cap, Contributed by Sherry Heit, Designed by Kirsten Kapur

0019 Wickery, Contributed by Patricia Would,
Cottonon, Designed by Woolly Wormhead

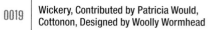

0020 Marble Muffin, Designed & Contributed
by Woolly Wormhead

0018 Crocheted Shells Tam, Designed & Contributed
by Rebecca Harmon

0021 | Bobble Beret, Designed & Contributed by Woolly Wormhead

0023 | Iola, Designed & Contributed by Katya Frankel

0024 | Pied Piper Tam, Designed & Contributed by Becka Rahn

0022 | Marina, Designed & Contributed by Woolly Wormhead

0026 | Kureyon Beret, Contributed by ChezPlum

0028 | Pumpkin Hat, Designed & Contributed by Marci Blank

0027 | Honeycomb Beret II, Designed & Contributed by Tricia Fagley

0025 | Disco Beret, Contributed by ChezPlum, Designed by Sylvie Damey

0031 | Urbane, Designed & Contributed by Katya Frankel

0029 | Woman's Beret, Contributed by Anne Blayney, Designed by Isabelle, purlbee.com

0030 | Tweed Beret, Contributed by Jill Packard, Designed by Kristen TenDyke

0034 | Beret, Contributed by
Maria Maxwell

0032 | Woman's Hat, Designed & Contributed
by Amy Pickard

0033 | Jaunty Cap, Designed & Contributed
by Terry Liann Morris

0035 | Morgan 2—Driving Cap, Designed &
Contributed by Anne Kuo Lukito

0036 | Felted Tam, Designed & Contributed by Elizabeth Carls

0038 | Women's Slouchy Ski Hat, Designed & Contributed by Tabitha Dick Oyediran, Knits So Divine

0037 | Concentric Circles Tam, Designed & Contributed by Rebecca Harmon

0039 | M, Contributed by Beth Rodio, Designed by Anne Kuo Lukito

0041 | Traversa, Contributed by Patricia Would, Cottonon, Designed by Woolly Wormhead

0042 | Cabled Cap, Contributed by Patricia Would, Cottonon, Designed by Woolly Wormhead

0040 | Purl Beret, Contributed by Rachel Kluesner, Designed by Isabelle, purlbee.com

Photo by Sungazing Photography

0043 | Viora, Designed & Contributed by Woolly Wormhead

0045 | Woman's Hat, Designed & Contributed by Zoë Valette

0047 | Alannah Hat, Contributed by Kristi L Knits, Designed by Kristi Founds

0044 | Chunky Smile Beret, Contributed by Tricia Fagley, Designed by Laurie Perry

0046 | Snowdrop Beret, Contributed by Sam Boice, Designed by Marya Spenton

0048 | Layla Tam, Designed & Contributed by Elizabeth Carls

0049 | Traversa, Designed & Contributed by Woolly Wormhead

0052 | Cabled Cap, Designed & Contributed by Woolly Wormhead

0054 | Tamya, Designed & Contributed by Woolly Wormhead

0053 | Short Row Beret, Contributed by ChezPlum, Designed by Sylvie Damey

0051 | Urchin Cap, Designed & Contributed by Woolly Wormhead

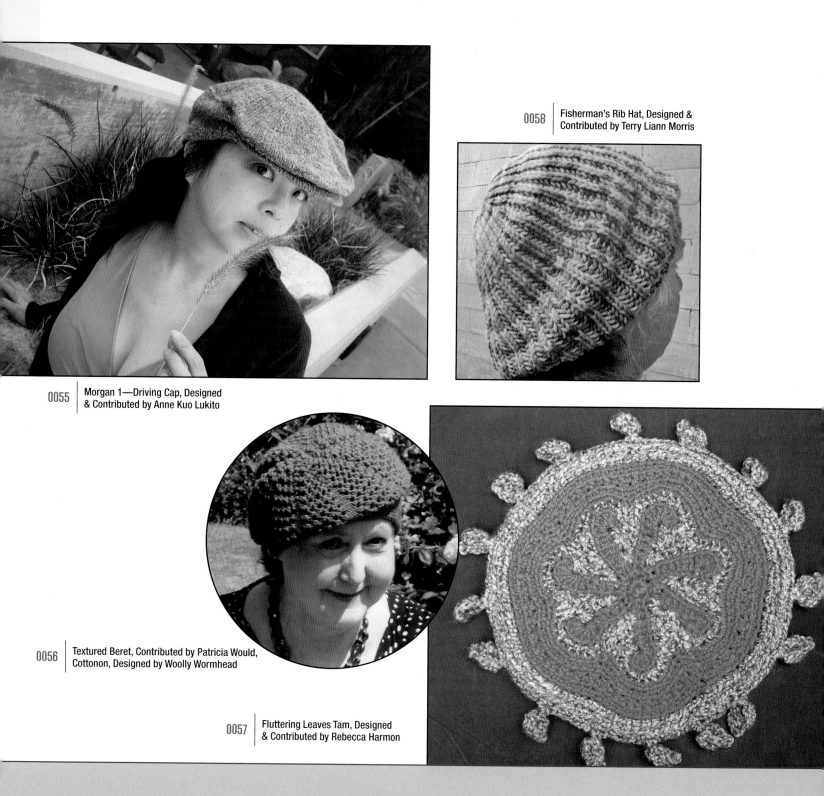

0058 | Fisherman's Rib Hat, Designed & Contributed by Terry Liann Morris

0055 | Morgan 1—Driving Cap, Designed & Contributed by Anne Kuo Lukito

0056 | Textured Beret, Contributed by Patricia Would, Cottonon, Designed by Woolly Wormhead

0057 | Fluttering Leaves Tam, Designed & Contributed by Rebecca Harmon

0060 | Gretchen's Dinner Plate, Designed & Contributed by Michelle Kennedy

0061 | Traversa & 2 Merets, Contributed by Yvonne Allen, Designed by Woolly Wormhead

0062 | Druidess Beret, Contributed by Constance M. Cole, Designed by Anna Bright

0059 | New Plaid Tam, Designed & Contributed by Margaret Hubert

Le Slouch, Contributed by Jessica Cheney,
Designed by Wendy Bernard

0066 Alice Paul, Designed &
Contributed by Anne Kuo Lukito

0064 The Newsboy, Designed & Contributed
by Margaret Hubert

0065 Tudor Cap, Contributed by Yvonne Allen,
Designed by Woolly Wormhead

0068 | Tonalita Woman's Cap, Designed &
Contributed by Shannita Williams-Alleyne

0069 | Striped Beret, Designed &
Contributed by Jasmine Davis

0067 | Tamarack, Designed & Contributed
by Amy M. Duncan

0070 | Garden Beret, Designed & Contributed
by Janel Laidman

0072 | Autumn Tam, Designed & Contributed
by Rebecca Harmon

0071 | Morgan 3—Driving Cap, Designed
& Contributed by Anne Kuo Lukito

0073 | Optimal Thinking Cap, Designed &
Contributed by Janel Laidman

0075 | Bubble Wrap Hat & Scarf, Designed &
Contributed by Tina Whitmore for Knitwhits

0074 | Pagoda Hat 2, Contributed by Kristi L Knits,
Designed by Kristi Founds

0078 | Sun Hat, Designed & Contributed by Mary Anne Cutler

0076 | Cowgirl Hat, Designed & Contributed by Lexi Boeger

0077 | Tassled Olive Cap, Designed & Contributed by Freyalyn Close-Hainsworth

0079 | Bee Hat, Designed & Contributed by Marci Blank

0081 | Big White, Designed & Contributed by Louise Gordon

0080 | Felted Big White, Designed & Contributed by Louise Gordon

0082 | Amanda Bucket, Designed & Contributed by Janice M Hamby, TwinSet Designs

0084 | Compass Rose Hat, Designed &
Contributed by Alasdair Post-Quinn

0085 | Summer Breeze Brimmed Hat, Designed
& Contributed by Margaret Hubert

0083 | Dissolve, Designed & Contributed by
Shannon Okey for knitgrrl.com

0086 | Reboux, Designed & Contributed by Shannon Okey for knitgrrl.com

0088 | Bucket Hat, Designed & Contributed by Katya Frankel

0087 | Abalone, Contributed by Yvonne Allen, Designed by Woolly Wormhead

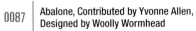

0089 | Oversized Greenie, Designed & Contributed by Louise Gordon

The Hats: Hat Shapes   **41**

0091 | Giggles Hat, Contributed by Ruth Bramley, Designed by Terry Liann Morris

0092 | Striped Drum, Designed & Contributed by Wanda Mitcham

0090 | Giggles Hat, Designed & Contributed by Terry Liann Morris

0094 | Woman's Hat, Designed & Contributed by Jane Nowakowski

0095 | Bella Hat, Designed & Contributed by Essie Woods Bruell

0093 | Peppermint Patty Hat, Designed & Contributed by Agnes Maderich, Hats by Agnes

0096 | Strudel, Designed & Contributed by Yvonne Allen

0097 | Trixie Winter Fling Hat, Designed & Contributed by Katie Harmon, PinkPolish Design

0098 | Striped Bucket, Designed & Contributed by Wanda Mitcham

0099 | Waves for Gravey, Designed & Contributed by Pam Pryshepa Ronan

0101 | Roll Brim Hat, Designed & Contributed by Marci Blank

0103 | Pinstripe, Designed & Contributed by Anne Kuo Lukito

0100 | A Better Bucket, Contributed by Jessica Cheney, Designed by Amy Swenson

0102 | Shades of Autumn Cap, Designed & Contributed by Rebecca Harmon

0105 | Skullie's Flowery Hat, Contributed by Copper Scale Dragon 2009, Designed by Jane Spaulding

0106 | Felted Cloche, Designed & Contributed by Elizabeth Carls

0104 | Karolina, Designed & Contributed by Harpa Jónsdóttir

0108 | Garter Stitch Hat, Designed
& Contributed by Marci Blank

0110 | Flowered Cloche, Designed &
Contributed by Katie Ahlquist

0107 | Grey Cabled Cloche, Designed
& Contributed by Rebecca Harmon

0109 | K&C Cloche, Designed &
Contributed by Mary Anne Cutler

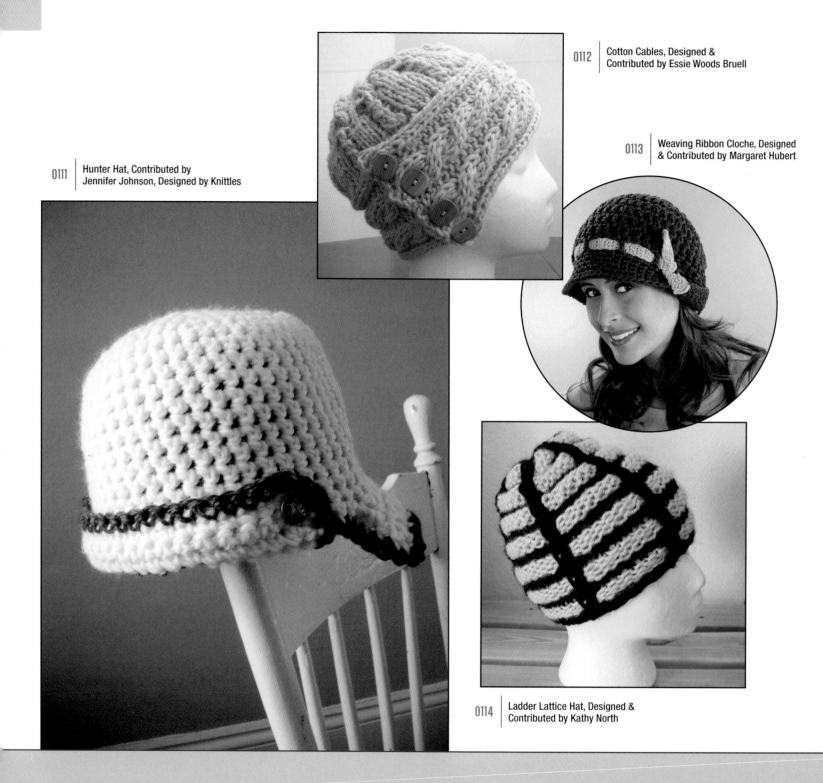

0112 | Cotton Cables, Designed & Contributed by Essie Woods Bruell

0112 | Cotton Cables, Designed & Contributed by Essie Woods Bruell

0113 | Weaving Ribbon Cloche, Designed & Contributed by Margaret Hubert

0111 | Hunter Hat, Contributed by Jennifer Johnson, Designed by Knittles

0114 | Ladder Lattice Hat, Designed & Contributed by Kathy North

0116 | Women's Cloche, Designed & Contributed by Anne Kuo Lukito

0117 | Silky Cloche, Designed & Contributed by Margaret Hubert

0115 | Mustard Floppy Flared Hat, Designed & Contributed by Lee Meredith

0118 | A Touch of Class, Designed & Contributed by Gunilla Buzzelli

0121 | Holiday Mystery Hood, Designed
& Contributed by Terry Liann Morris

0119 | Button Balaclava, Designed & Contributed
by Agnes Maderich, Hats by Agnes

0120 | Cotton Candy Scarf Hat, Designed
& Contributed by Margaret Hubert

0123 | Black Knight Hood, Designed
& Contributed by Annie Modesitt

0122 | Blue Face Mask, Designed &
Contributed by Annie Modesitt

0124 | Pfeiffer Falls, Designed & Contributed
by Anne Kuo Lukito

0126 | Striped Balaclava, Contributed by Carolyn Vance, Designed by Helen Fleischer

0127 | Sutton Who?, Designed & Contributed by Annie Modesitt

0128 | Blue Mask, Designed & Contributed by Annie Modesitt

0125 | Tom's Balaclava, Contributed by Carolyn Vance, Designed by Helen Fleischer

0131 | Electrochok, Designed &
Contributed by Brittany Wilson

0129 | Fuzz Hood, Designed
& Contributed by Marci Blank

0130 | Roadside Gerry Ski Mask, Designed
& Contributed by Annie Modesitt

0133 | Hand-Dyed Berries Vortex, Designed & Contributed by Lee Meredith

0134 | Triangle Tassle Cap, Designed & Contributed by Freyalyn Close-Hainsworth

0132 | Twisted, Designed & Contributed by Gunilla Buzzelli

0135 | Head Wrap with Petal Frill, Designed & Contributed by Sharon Menges

0137 | Woman's Hat, Designed & Contributed
by Jeri Robinson-Lawrence, Flying Fibers

0136 | Woman's Hat, Designed & Contributed
by Jeri Robinson-Lawrence, Flying Fibers

0138 | Let's Twist, Designed &
Contributed by Gunilla Buzzelli

0140 | Flapper Hat, Designed & Contributed by Gunilla Buzzelli

0141 | Crochet Möbius 3, Designed & Contributed by Mary Anne Cutler

0139 | Crochet Möbius Hat, Designed & Contributed by Mary Anne Cutler

0142 | Pleated Beret, Designed & Contributed by Woolly Wormhead

0143 | Calorimetry, Contributed by Agnes Maderich,
Hats by Agnes, Designed by Kathryn Schoendorf

0144 | Celtic Head Wrap, Designed
& Contributed by Sharon Menges

0145 | Crochet Möbius 2, Designed
& Contributed by Mary Anne Cutler

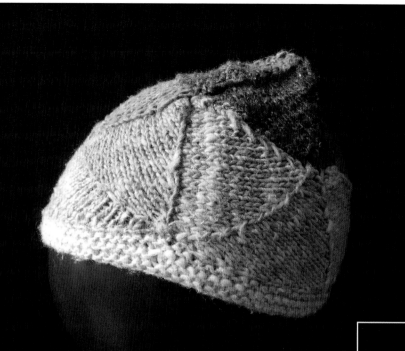

0146 | Modular Triangle Hat 1,
Designed & Contributed by Mari Tobita

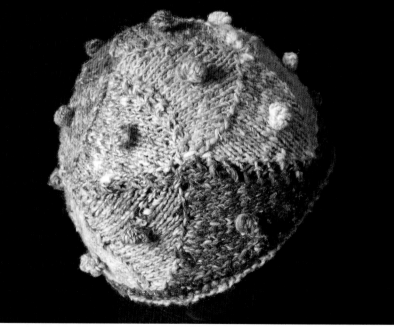

0147 | Modular Triangle Hat 2,
Designed & Contributed by Mari Tobita

0149 | Helmet, Contributed by Katie Ahlquist,
Designed by Angela Juergens

0150 | Elfin Hat, Contributed by Katie Ahlquist,
Designed by Sonya Laska

0151 | Kitty Hat, Contributed by Sam Boice,
Designed by Lisa Whiting

0153 | Seussical Hat, Contributed by Sue Caldwell,
Lovely Yarns, Designed by Saartje Bruin

0152 | Warmth for Those Who Have Little, Designed &
Contributed by Anne Blayney

0154 | Poof, Contributed by the SWTC Collection,
Designed by Joan Somerville

0155 | Altay Pink, Contributed by ChezPlum,
Designed by Sylvie Damey

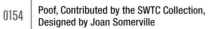

0156 The Amanda Hat, Contributed by
Kathleen Conery, Designed by Gina House

0157 Ribba Again, Designed &
Contributed by Woolly Wormhead

0158 Flappy Cabler, Designed &
Contributed by Woolly Wormhead

0159 | Cat Hat, Designed & Contributed by Anne Kuo Lukito

0161 | Peacock Bonnet, Designed & Contributed by Cosette Cornelius-Bates

0160 | Slouch Hat, Designed & Contributed by Lexi Boeger

0162 | Warmth for Those Who Have Little,
Designed & Contributed by Anne Blayney

0165 | Frostroses, Designed &
Contributed by Harpa Jónsdóttir

0163 | Warmth for Those Who Have Little,
Designed & Contributed by Anne Blayney

0164 | Bjïrg, Designed &
Contributed by Harpa Jónsdóttir

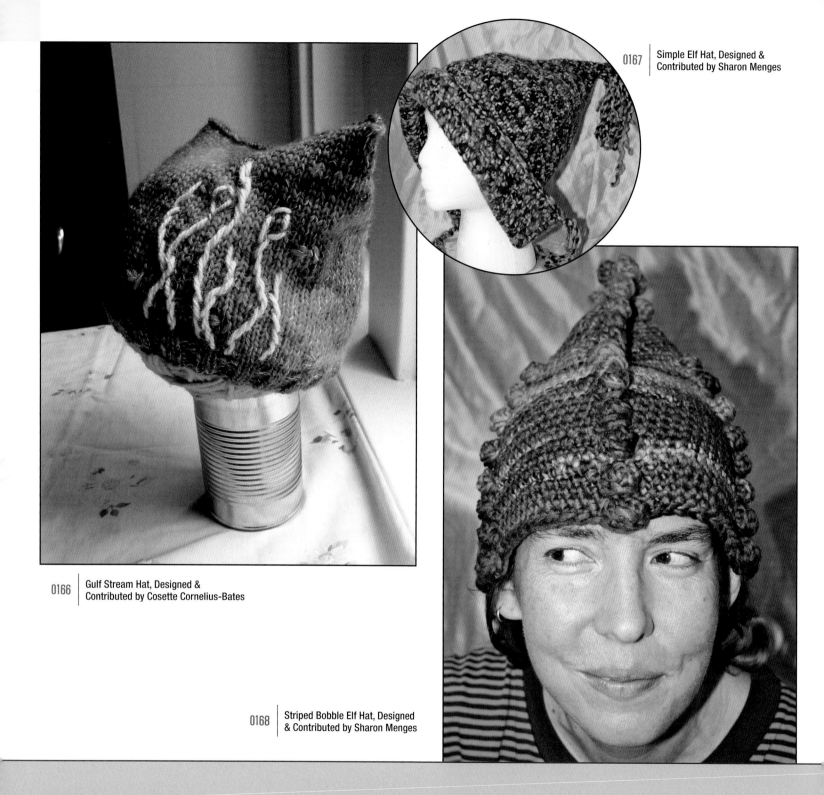

0167 | Simple Elf Hat, Designed & Contributed by Sharon Menges

0166 | Gulf Stream Hat, Designed & Contributed by Cosette Cornelius-Bates

0168 | Striped Bobble Elf Hat, Designed & Contributed by Sharon Menges

0169   Ganomy Hat, Contributed by Mandy Powers,
       Designed by Elizabeth Zimmerman

0171   Two by One Hat, Designed
       & Contributed by Mandy Powers

0170   Fabulous Hat, Designed &
       Contributed by Annie Modesitt

0172   All Things Grow Hat, Designed &
       Contributed by Cosette Cornelius-Bates

0173 | A Pair, Designed & Contributed by Harpa Jónsdóttir

0174 | Unisex Hat, Designed & Contributed by Josi Hannon Madera, Art of Crochet

0175 | Sand, Designed & Contributed by Harpa Jónsdóttir

0177 | Ribba Cap, Designed & Contributed by Woolly Wormhead

0176 | Sloochie (Pixie Version), Designed & Contributed by Woolly Wormhead

0178 | Earflap Hat, Contributed by ChezPlum, Designed by Sylvie Damey

0179 | Pom-Pom Hat, Contributed by ChezPlum, Designed by Sylvie Damey

0183 | Blendy Striped Haka, Designed
& Contributed by Lee Meredith

0180 | Technicolor Unicorn, Designed
& Contributed by Wanda Mitcham

0181 | Elf Hat, Designed & Contributed
by Pam Pryshepa Ronan

0182 | A Bonnet to Dream In, Designed
& Contributed by Cosette Cornelius-Bates

0184 | Jester's Cap, Designed & Contributed by Rebecca Harmon

0185 | Dobby Hat, Contributed by Sam Boice, Designed by Sarah Hasse

0186 | Julia's Hat, Contributed by Carolyn Vance, Designed by Dawn Adcock

0189 | Witch's Hat and Cat, Contributed by
Mandy Furney, Designed by Cheryl Oxsalida

0188 | Rainbow Elf, Designed & Contributed
by Louise Gordon

0190 | Ribba, Contributed by Patricia Would,
Cottonon, Designed by Woolly Wormhead

0192 | Little Warrior Hat, Designed & Contributed by Galina Fedtchenko

0191 | Flap Happy, Contributed by Carolyn Vance, Designed by Susan B. Anderson

0193 | Sponge Bob, Contributed by ChezPlum

0195 | Maltese Fisherman's Hat, Contributed by Agnes Maderich, Hats by Agnes, Designed by Elizabeth Zimmerman

0197 | Samui Toque, Designed & Contributed by Kendra Nitta

0194 | Furry Hat, Designed & Contributed by Marci Blank

0196 | Bobble Hat, Designed & Contributed by Sharon Menges

0199   Official Kittyville Hat, Contributed by
Ellen M. Silva, Designed by Kitty Schmidt

0198   Woman's Hat, Contributed by Kelli Nottingham,
Designed by Judith L. Swartz

0200   Tassel Hat, Designed &
Contributed by Marci Blank

0204 | Kitty Hat, Contributed by Sam
Boice, Designed by Lisa Whiting

0201 | Fabulous Hats, Designed
& Contributed by Annie Modesitt

0202 | Ganomy Hat, Contributed by Mandy Powers,
Designed by Elizabeth Zimmerman

0203 | Pointy Ear Bulky, Designed
& Contributed by Anne Kuo Lukito

0206   Mini Hat, Designed & Contributed
by Anne Kuo Lukito

0207   Kitty Ear Hat, Designed &
Contributed by Alexandra Johnson

0208   Purple Twist Bobble Hat,
Designed & Contributed by Sharon Menges

0205   Handspun Hat, Designed & Contributed by
Janine Le Cras, Guernseygal Designs

0211 | Owl Hat, Designed & Contributed by Melissa LaBarre

0209 | Simple Stuff Beanie, Designed & Contributed by Margaret Hubert

0210 | Girl Beanie, Designed & Contributed by Margaret Hubert

0212 | Norse Goddess, Contributed by Katie Ahlquist, Designed by Lucy Mackenzie & Kirsteen Mitcalfe

0214 | Constellations, Designed & Contributed by Tori Seierstad, Torirot Design

0213 | Butterflies, Designed & Contributed by Harpa Jónsdóttir

0215 | Urbanista, Designed & Contributed by Woolly Wormhead

0216 | Ganomy Hat, Contributed by Lorraine Ehrlinger Designs, Designed by Elizabeth Zimmerman

0218 | Woman's Hat, Contributed by Sandra Benward

0219 | Confetti Hat, Designed & Contributed by Marci Blank

0217 | Cashmere Watch, Designed & Contributed by Agnes Maderich, Hats by Agnes

0220 | Beaded Woman's Hat,
Designed & Contributed by Beth Callahan

0222 | Watch Cap, Contributed
by Louise Gordon

0221 | Rolled Brim Hat 1, Designed & Contributed by
Sarah E. White, knitting.about.com

0223 | Harris Hat, Contributed by Deborah Heinzle,
Designed by Jane Ellison

0225 | Russian Hat, Designed & Contributed by Terry Liann Morris

0226 | Bree, Designed & Contributed by Brittany Wilson

0224 | Hat Collection, Designed & Contributed by Tina Whitmore for Knitwhits

0228 | Moscow Hat, Designed &
Contributed by Terry Liann Morris

0227 | Rachel's Space Hat, Contributed by Agnes
Maderich, Hats by Agnes, Designed by Rachel Behm

0229 | Funky Flapper, Designed &
Contributed by Woolly Wormhead

0232 Dylan's Beanie, Contributed by Patricia Would, Cottonon, Designed by Woolly Wormhead

0231 Icelandic Garter Hat, Designed & Contributed by Charisa Martin Cairn

0233 Felted Bowler, Contributed by Maria Maxwell

0230 Glœmosi, Designed & Contributed by Harpa Jónsdóttir

0234 | Unoriginal Hat, Contributed by Ruth Moline,
Designed by Stephanie Pearl-McPhee

0236 | Gansey Gayle, Contributed by Kimberly Lewis,
Designed by Terry Liann Morris

0235 | Man's Hat, Contributed by Anne Blayney,
Designed by Vanessa Ewing

0237 | Eighty Percent, Designed
& Contributed by Sarah Fay

0239 | WVU Mountaineer Hat, Designed & Contributed by Susie Slider

0240 | Recycled Handspun Art Hat, Designed & Contributed by Lee Meredith

0238 | Hat Collection, Designed & Contributed by Tina Whitmore for Knitwhits

0241 | Handspun Bonnet, Designed & Contributed by Lee Meredith

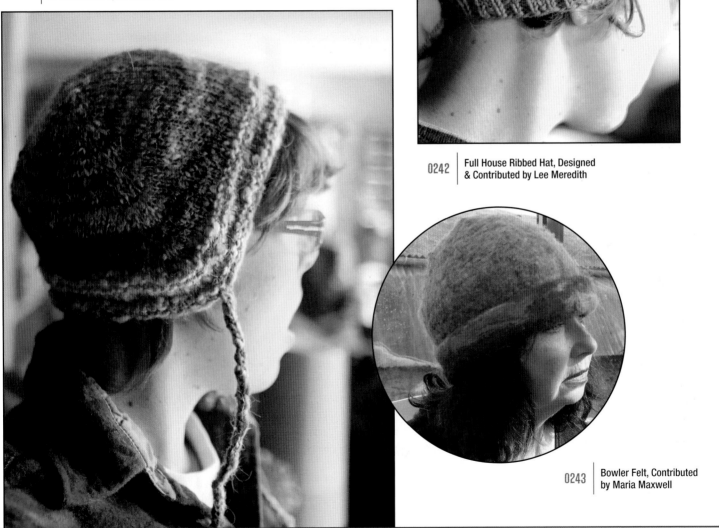

0242 | Full House Ribbed Hat, Designed & Contributed by Lee Meredith

0243 | Bowler Felt, Contributed by Maria Maxwell

0245 | Watch Cap, Contributed by M Kathryn
Adkins, Designed by Elizabeth Zimmerman

0246 | Noodle Cozy, Designed & Contributed
by Laura Martos of Dizzy Blonde Studios

0244 | Mega Beaded Hat, Designed
& Contributed by Kathy North

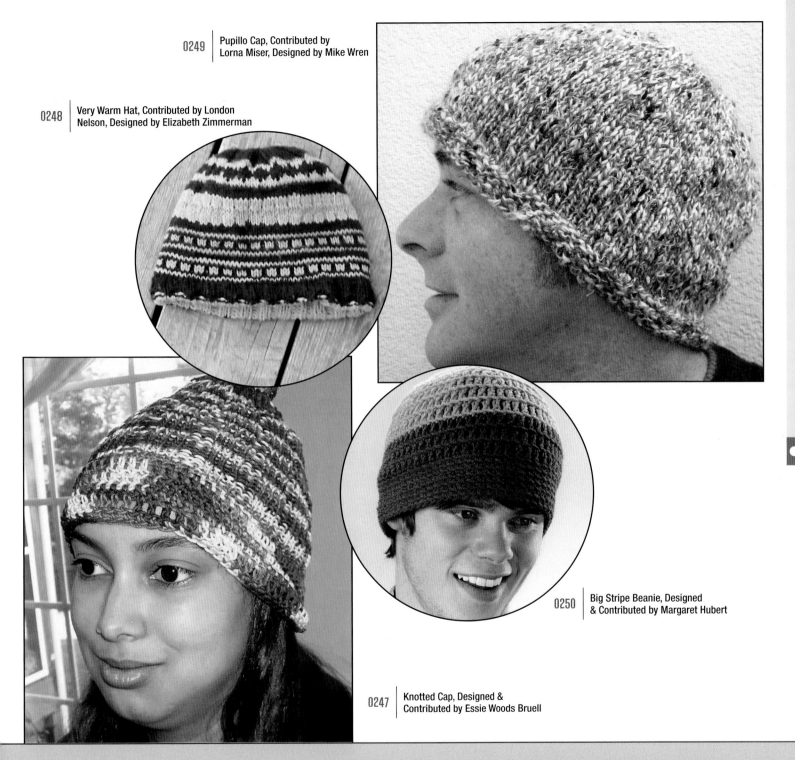

0249 Pupillo Cap, Contributed by
Lorna Miser, Designed by Mike Wren

0248 Very Warm Hat, Contributed by London
Nelson, Designed by Elizabeth Zimmerman

0250 Big Stripe Beanie, Designed
& Contributed by Margaret Hubert

0247 Knotted Cap, Designed &
Contributed by Essie Woods Bruell

0253 | Noma, Designed &
Contributed by Woolly Wormhead

0252 | Flower Hat, Designed &
Contributed by Maddie Pollis

0251 | Miniature Toque, Designed & Contributed
by Agnes Maderich, Hats by Agnes

0254 | Beaded Woman's Hat, Designed
& Contributed by Beth Callahan

0255 | Thorpe Hat, Contributed by Mandy Powers, Designed by Kirsten Kapur

0258 | Thorpe Earflap Hat, Contributed by Constance M. Cole, Designed by Kirsten Kapur

0256 | Seaman's Hat, Contributed by Brenda Cunningham, Designed by Brenda Zuk

0257 | Armenian Hat, Contributed by Carolyn Vance, Designed by Meg Swanson

0260 | I'll Pack a Hat, Designed & Contributed by Joanne Seiff

0261 | Perfect Guy Hat, Designed & Contributed by Michelle Kennedy

0259 | Man Hat, Contributed by Angela Tong, Designed by Brenda Zuk

0262 | Lotsa Hats, Contributed by Carolyn Vance

0263 | Icelandic Winter Cap, Designed & Contributed by Joanne Seiff

0264 | Felted Twined Bowler, Designed & Contributed by Carolyn Vance

0265 | Peruvian Watch, Designed & Contributed by Agnes Maderich, Hats by Agnes

0266 | Ski Bonnet, Designed & Contributed by Agnes Maderich, Hats by Agnes

0267 | Teeny Tiny Snow Hat, Designed & Contributed by Julie Witt

0268 | Hot Textures Hat, Designed & Contributed by Margaret Hubert

0269 | Red Bobble Hat, Designed & Contributed by Susie Slider

0270 | Ribbed Flat Hat, Contributed by Sarah E. White, knitting.about.com, Designed by Sarah E. White

0271 | Amelia Earhart, Designed
& Contributed by Anne Kuo Lukito

0272 | Poodle Cap, Designed &
Contributed by Margaret Hubert

0273 | Loopy Flapper, Contributed by Patricia Would,
Cottonon, Designed by Woolly Wormhead

0275 | Throwback Helmet Hat, Designed & Contributed by Mandy Powers

0276 | SOAR Hat, Designed & Contributed by Cosette Cornelius-Bates

0274 | How I Met Your Mother Hat, Designed & Contributed by Lee Meredith

0277 | Subtle Stripes Hat, Designed & Contributed by Cosette Cornelius-Bates

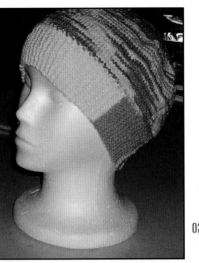

0279 | Stripes & Colorblock, Contributed by Sandra Benward, Designed by Debbi Young

0278 | Gryffindor Doublemassa, Designed & Contributed by Lisa Putnam

0280 | Sea Glass Hat, Designed & Contributed by Brittany Wilson

0282 Reversing Stripes, Designed
& Contributed by Tori Seierstad,
Torirot Design

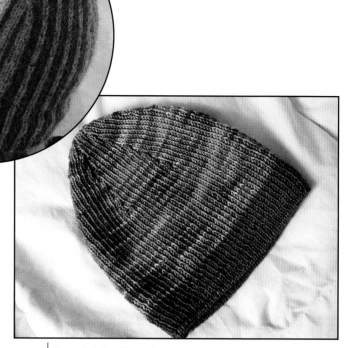

0283 | Pismo Hat, Contributed by Anne Blayney,
Designed by Marnie MacLean

0281 | Colored Lozenges, Designed
& Contributed by Tricia Pendergrass

0284 | Simple Man's Hat, Contributed by
Rebecca Mercier, Designed by Andrea & Amy Mielke

0286 | Paul's Hat, Designed & Contributed by Anne Blayney

0287 | Spiral Striped Toque, Contributed by Constance M. Cole

0285 | Four Corner Hat, Contributed by Anne Crawford, Designed by Maureen Mason Jamieson

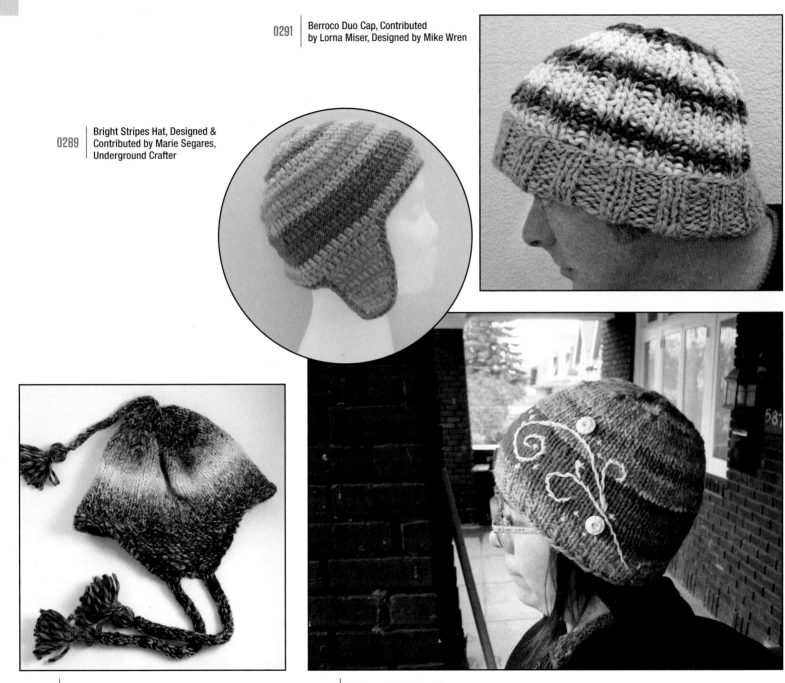

0291   Berroco Duo Cap, Contributed by Lorna Miser, Designed by Mike Wren

0289   Bright Stripes Hat, Designed & Contributed by Marie Segares, Underground Crafter

0288   Grey Flap Hat, Contributed by Tricia Fagley

0290   Flurries Hat, Designed & Contributed by Cosette Cornelius-Bates

0292 | Handspun Angora Hat, Contributed by
Lorna Miser, Designed by Mike Wren

0294 | Izzy Hat & Scarf, Designed &
Contributed by Tina Whitmore
for Knitwhits

0293 | Noro Hat, Contributed by Anne Crawford,
Designed by Saartje Bruin

0298 | Second Beanie with Noro, Designed & Contributed by Terry Liann Morris

0300 | Cable Hat, Designed & Contributed by Marci Blank

0299 | Beanies with Noro, Designed & Contributed by Terry Liann Morris

0301 | Reverse Stockinette Stitch Hat, Designed & Contributed by Mandy Powers

0303 | Colored Lozenges,
Contributed by Sandra Benward

0302 | Woman's Hat, Designed & Contributed by
Josi Hannon Madera, Art of Crochet

0304 | The Amanda Hat, Contributed by
Caroline Conery, Designed by Gina House

0305 | Charity Hat, Designed &
Contributed by AnneLena K. Mattison

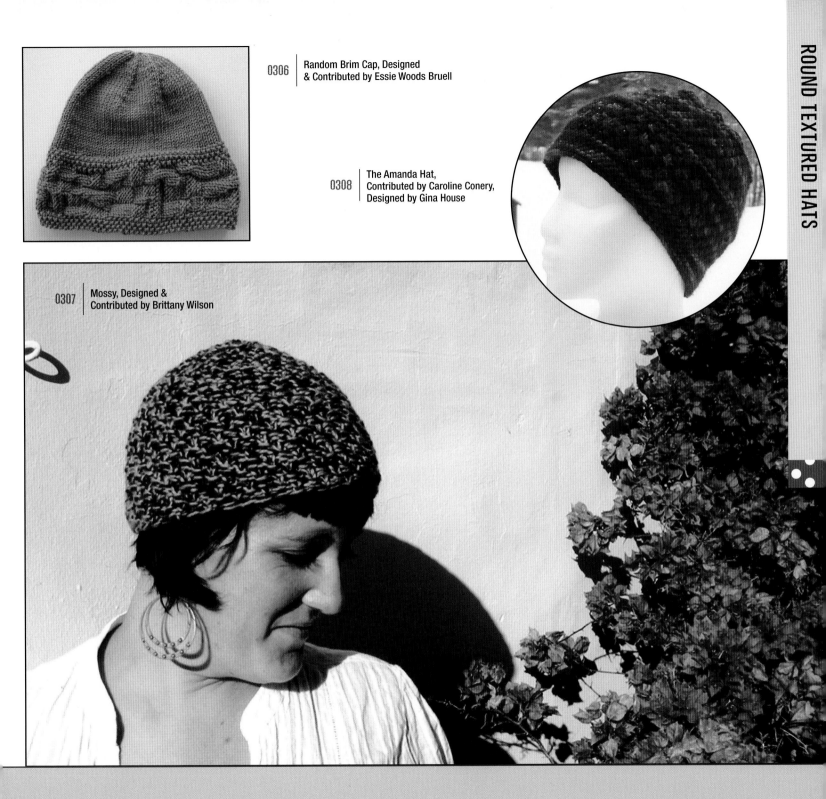

0306 | Random Brim Cap, Designed
& Contributed by Essie Woods Bruell

0308 | The Amanda Hat,
Contributed by Caroline Conery,
Designed by Gina House

0307 | Mossy, Designed &
Contributed by Brittany Wilson

0310 Folk Art for Your Head, Designed & Contributed by Charisa Martin Cairn

0312 Lace Beareanie, Contributed by Brenda Cunningham, Designed by Gunilla Leavitt

0311 Chapeau Marnier, Contributed by Anne Blayney, Designed by Marnie MacLean

0309 The Amanda Hat, Contributed by Caroline Conery, Designed by Gina House

0314 | Gartered Garden Hat, Designed
& Contributed by Terry Liann Morris

0313 | One Row Tweed Stripe Hat, Designed
& Contributed by Kathy North

0315 | The Amanda Hat, Contributed by
Jacqueline Wolk, Designed by Gina House

0317 | Saddle Hat, Designed & Contributed by Agnes Maderich, Hats by Agnes

0316 | Alpaca Karoke Cap, Designed & Contributed by Sherria Tyler

0318 | Slightly Loopy, Designed & Contributed by Woolly Wormhead

0320 | Experimental Houses Hat, Designed
& Contributed by Lee Meredith

0321 | Colourscape Hat, Designed
& Contributed by Tricia Fagley

0322 | Really Warm Hat, Designed
& Contributed by Melissa LaBarre

0319 | Ocean Breeze, Designed & Contributed
by Lee Meredith

0324 | Woman's Hat, Designed & Contributed by
Cheryl Savage, Squirrels' Nest

0323 | Braid Hat, Designed
& Contributed by Lexi Boeger

0325 | Twined Knitted Cap, Designed
& Contributed by Rebecca Harmon

0327 | Checkerboard Hat, Designed
& Contributed by Lois Ellen Designs

0328 | Quaker Ribbed Brim Hat, Designed
& Contributed by Rebecca Mercier

0326 | Slouchy Short Row, Designed
& Contributed by Brittany Wilson

0329 | Colorful Rib Cap, Designed
& Contributed by Rebecca Harmon

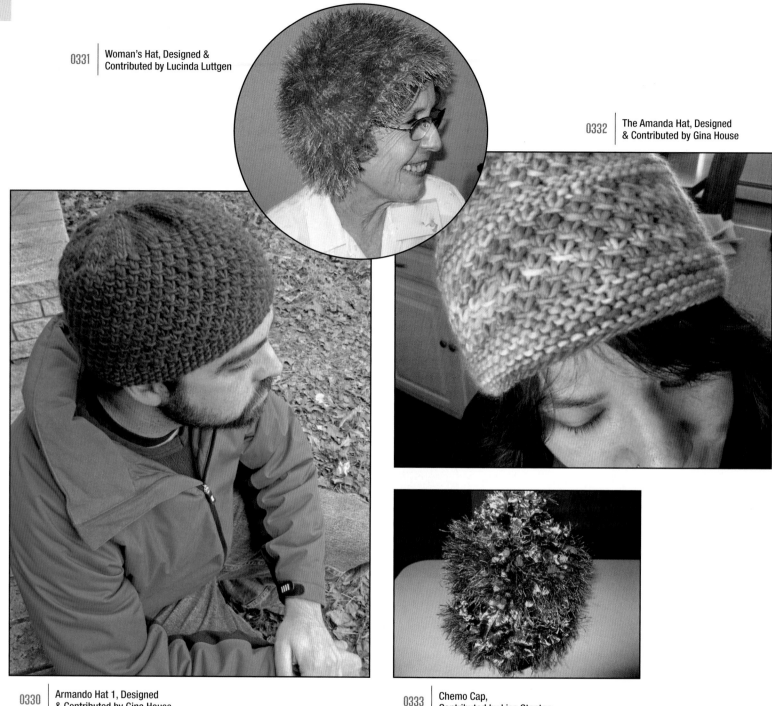

0331 | Woman's Hat, Designed & Contributed by Lucinda Luttgen

0332 | The Amanda Hat, Designed & Contributed by Gina House

0330 | Armando Hat 1, Designed & Contributed by Gina House

0333 | Chemo Cap, Contributed by Lisa Stanton

0337 | Diamond Grid Hat,
Contributed by Deborah Heinzle,
Designed by Jared Flood

0335 | Armando Hat 3, Designed
& Contributed by Gina House

0334 | Buckle Striped Hat, Designed
& Contributed by Mary Keenan

0336 | Askew, Designed &
Contributed by Brittany Wilson

The Hats: Hat Shapes   111

0339 | The Amanda Hat,
Contributed by Marion Conery,
Designed by Gina House

0341 | Brick Hat, Designed &
Contributed by Stephanie Voyer

0340 | The Amanda Hat, Contributed by
Caroline Conery, Designed by Gina House

0338 | Roll-Brim Hat, Designed
& Contributed by Margaret Hubert

0342 | Cable Fabric Hat, Designed
& Contributed by Susie Slider

0343 | The Amanda Hat,
Contributed by Caroline Conery,
Designed by Gina House

0344 | Unisex Hat, Designed & Contributed by
Josi Hannon Madera, Art of Crochet

0346 | Retro Fold-Top Hat, Designed &
Contributed by Essie Woods Bruell

0347 | Seed Stitch Hat, Designed
& Contributed by Marci Blank

0345 | The Amanda Hat, Designed
& Contributed by Gina House

0348 | Max in Ice Pouf, Designed & Contributed
by Janice M. Hamby, TwinSet Designs

0350 | The Amanda Hat, Contributed by
ErickaJo Haddad, Designed by Gina House

0351 | The Amanda Hat, Contributed by
Jacqueline Wolk, Designed by Gina House

0349 | The Amanda Hat, Designed
& Contributed by Gina House

0352 | Silky Silvery Cap, Designed
& Contributed by Rebecca Harmon

0353 | River Pebbles, Designed
& Contributed by Lois Ellen Designs

0354 | Secret Agent, Contributed
by Sandra Benward

0356 | Fake Fur Hat, Designed &
Contributed by Lorna Miser

0357 | Eyelash Hat, Designed &
Contributed by Marci Blank

0355 | The Amanda Hat, Contributed by
Caroline Conery, Designed by Gina House

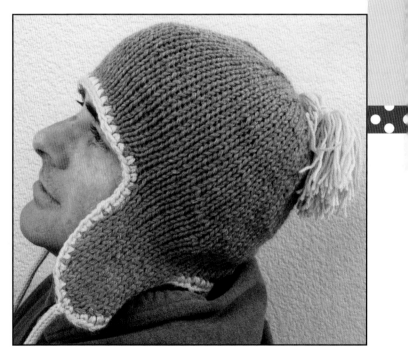

0358 | Acrylic Stash Cap, Contributed by
Lorna Miser, Designed by Mike Wren

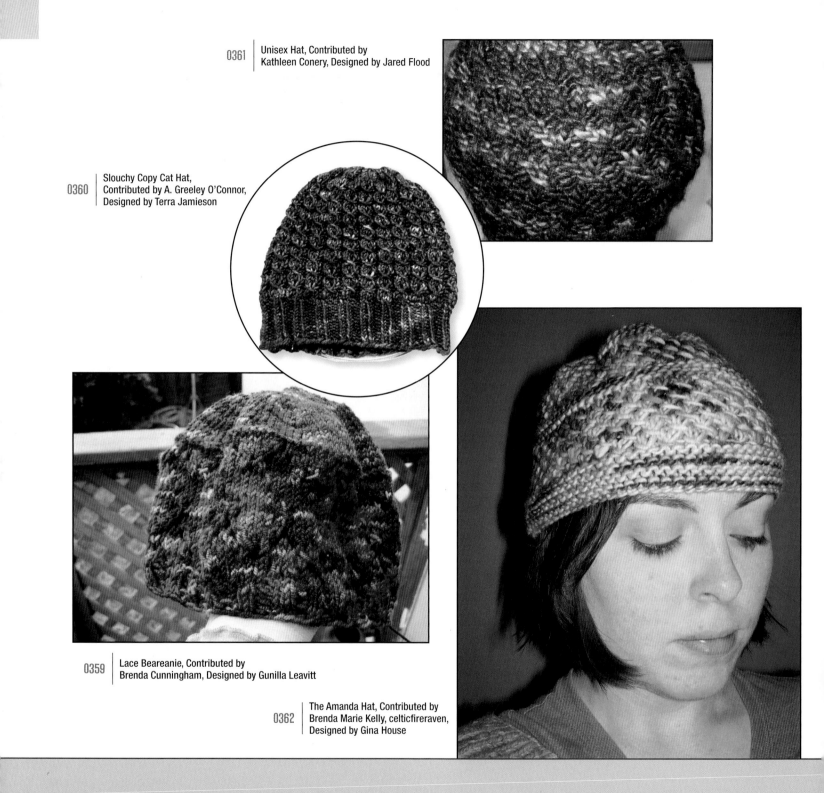

0361 | Unisex Hat, Contributed by
Kathleen Conery, Designed by Jared Flood

0360 | Slouchy Copy Cat Hat,
Contributed by A. Greeley O'Connor,
Designed by Terra Jamieson

0359 | Lace Beareanie, Contributed by
Brenda Cunningham, Designed by Gunilla Leavitt

0362 | The Amanda Hat, Contributed by
Brenda Marie Kelly, celticfireraven,
Designed by Gina House

0364 | Uninspired Hat, Contributed by
A.M., Designed by Stephanie
Pearl-McPhee

0365 | Acrylic Stash Hat, Designed
& Contributed by Lorna Miser

0366 | Koolhaas, Contributed by Anne Crawford,
Designed by Jared Flood

0363 | The Amanda Hat, Contributed by
Jacqueline Wolk, Designed by Gina House

0368 | Craft Hat, Contributed by the SWTC Collection, Designed by Vickie Howell

0370 | Harvest Watchcap, Contributed by A.M.

0367 | Armando Hat 2, Designed & Contributed by Gina House

0369 | Gansey Gayle Hat, Designed & Contributed by Terry Liann Morris

0371 | Ridge Brim Hat, Designed & Contributed by Essie Woods Bruell

0374 | Dulaan Avalanche Hat, Contributed by Kathleen Conery, Designed by Ryan Morris

0372 | Baby Pumpkin Hat, Designed & Contributed by Sarah E. White, knitting .about.com

0373 | Checker Block Hat, Designed & Contributed by Lois Ellen Designs

0376 | Dark, Seedy & Twisted, Designed & Contributed by Sharon Hanson

0377 | The Amanda Hat, Contributed by Caroline Conery, Designed by Gina House

0375 | The Amanda Hat, Contributed by Jacqueline Wolk, Designed by Gina House

0379 | Simple Stitches, Designed & Contributed by Essie Woods Bruell

0380 | The Amanda Hat, Contributed by Caroline Conery, Designed by Gina House

0378 | The Amanda Hat, Contributed by Caroline Conery, Designed by Gina House

0381 | Free to Dream, Contributed by the SWTC Collection, Designed by Jonelle Raffino

The Hats: Hat Shapes   123

0383 | The Amanda Hat, Contributed by Brenda Marie Kelly, celticfireraven, Designed by Gina House

0382 | Quincy, Contributed by Yvonne Allen, Designed by Jared Flood

0384 | Short Rows Wavy Hat, Contributed by Yvonne Allen, Designed by Lee Meredith

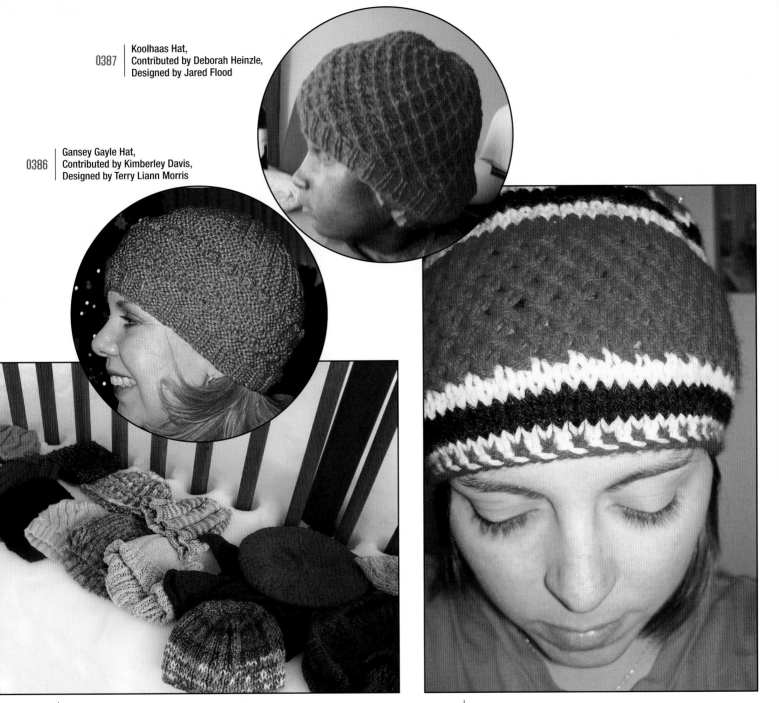

0387 | Koolhaas Hat,
Contributed by Deborah Heinzle,
Designed by Jared Flood

0386 | Gansey Gayle Hat,
Contributed by Kimberley Davis,
Designed by Terry Liann Morris

0385 | Variety of Hats, Contributed by
Constance M. Cole, Designed by Various

0388 | The Amanda Hat, Contributed by Brenda Marie Kelly,
celticfireraven, Designed by Gina House

0389 | Tibetan Temple, Designed &
Contributed by Andrea L. Stern

0390 | Alice's Repose, Designed &
Contributed by Andrea L. Stern

0391 | Donald, Designed &
Contributed by Andrea L. Stern

0393 | Lion's Mane Hood, Designed & Contributed by Margaret Hubert

0394 | Butt Quack, Designed & Contributed by Laura Martos of Dizzy Blonde Studios

0392 | Mini Sombrero, Designed & Contributed by Lynn Johanna, Lady Willow Designs

Photo by LadyWillow

0395 | Fish Hat, Contributed by Lisa Stanton, Designed by Thelma Egbert

0397 Softserve Coiled Hat, Designed & Contributed by Lexi Boeger

0398 A Walk in the Forest, Designed & Contributed by Andrea L. Stern

0396 Dog Ski Hat, Designed & Contributed by Emily Allison

0399 Top Hat, Contributed by Yvonne Allen, Designed by Tami Chapman

0401 | Beehive Hat,
Contributed by Carolyn Vance

0402 | Mini Toucan, Designed & Contributed by Lynn Johanna,
Lady Willow Designs

Photo by LadyWillow

0400 | Foliage Hat, Designed &
Contributed by Sharon Menges

Temple in the Clouds, Designed & Contributed by Andrea L. Stern

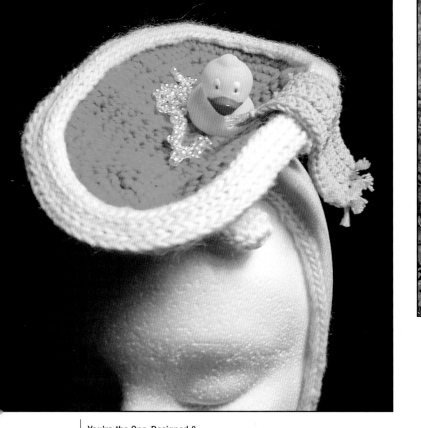

0405 | High Hat, Contributed by ChezPlum, Designed by Sylvie Damey

0403 | You're the One, Designed & Contributed by Andrea L. Stern

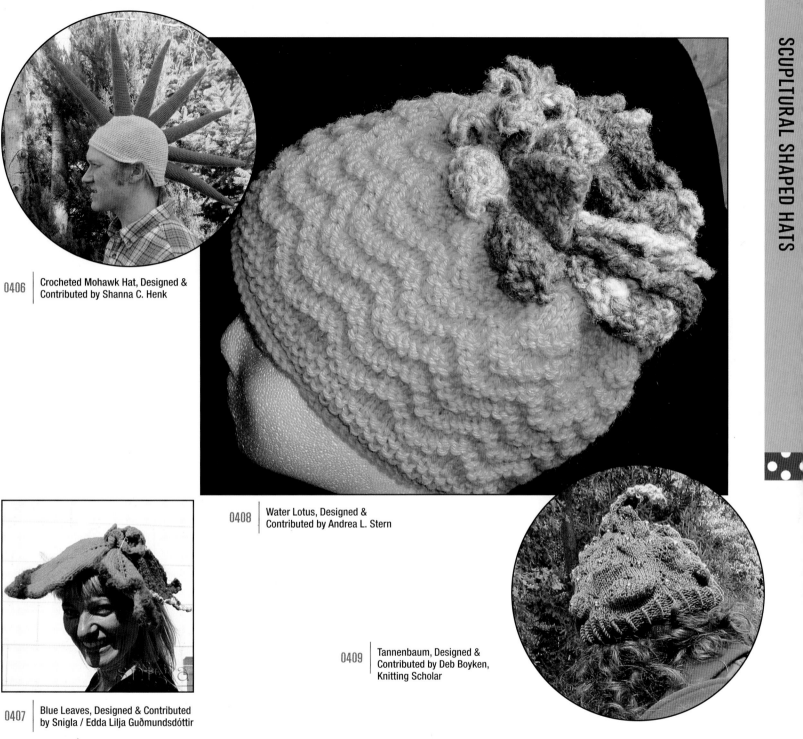

0406 | Crocheted Mohawk Hat, Designed &
Contributed by Shanna C. Henk

0408 | Water Lotus, Designed &
Contributed by Andrea L. Stern

0409 | Tannenbaum, Designed &
Contributed by Deb Boyken,
Knitting Scholar

0407 | Blue Leaves, Designed & Contributed
by Snigla / Edda Lilja Guðmundsdóttir

0411 | Cowboy Hat,
Contributed by Ruth Moline

0410 | Knit Motorcycle Cap, Designed &
Contributed by Annie Modesitt

0412 | Witch's Hat Collection, Contributed by
Mandy Furney, Designed by Cheryl Oxsalida

0415 | Ermine Hat, Designed &
Contributed by Selina Siu
Photo by Kristina Sinzig

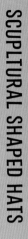

0416 | Klein Bottle Hat,
Designed & Contributed by
Sarah-Marie Belcastro

0414 | Bird's Nest Hat, Designed &
Contributed by Michelle Kennedy

0418 | Dog Ski Hat, Designed &
Contributed by Emily Allison

0419 | Bad Hair Day Mohican Hat,
Designed & Contributed by Ruth Bramley

0417 | Wall St. Trollop, Designed &
Contributed by Yvonne Allen

0421 | Entrelac with Baseball, Contributed by Toni Blye, Designed by It's Curious

0422 | Camo Hat, Designed & Contributed by Sarah E. White, knitting.about.com,

0420 | Ghost Town Zombie Hat, Designed & Contributed by Lexi Boeger

0423 | Gold-Tipped Drum, Designed & Contributed by Wanda Mitcham

0425 | Nest, Designed & Contributed by Andrea L. Stern

0424 | Flore Petal Hats, Designed & Contributed by Tina Whitmore for Knitwhits

0426 | Chicken Butt, Contributed by Tanya L. Seidman, Designed by Ariel Marie Seidman

0428 | Hallowig, Contributed by Shanna C. Henk, Designed by Megan Reardon

0427 | Pillbox Hat, Designed & Contributed by Lexi Boeger

0429 | Hat Ornament, Contributed by Angela Tong, Designed by Susan B. Anderson

0430 | Entrelac Hat, Contributed by Toni Blye,
Designed by It's Curious

0432 | Bell the Cat, Designed &
Contributed by Michelle Kennedy

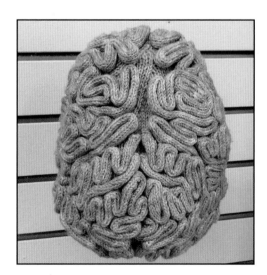

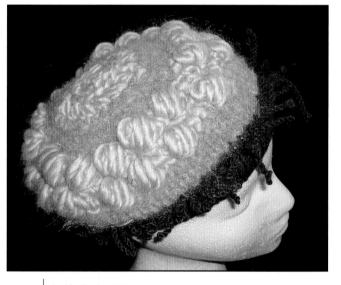

0431 | Brain Hat, Designed &
Contributed by Marti Fuerst

0433 | Jackie, Designed &
Contributed by Andrea L. Stern

0435 | Let Them Eat Cake, Designed & Contributed by Andrea L. Stern

0436 | Fedora, Contributed by Yvonne Allen, Designed by Tami Chapman

0434 | Dragon Butt Hat, Designed & Contributed by Diana Troldahl

0438 | Ariosa Pom-Pom Hat, Contributed by
Sam Boice, Designed by Hannah Fettig

0439 | X & O Stocking Cap,
Contributed by Maria Maxwell

0440 | Elf Hat, Designed &
Contributed by Marci Blank

0437 | Whimsey, Contributed by Rachel Kluesner,
Designed by Dyeabolical Yarns

Photo by Sungazing Photography

0442 | Rustic Stocking Hat, Designed & Contributed by Alicia McLemore Bal

0441 | 10 Below Hat, Contributed by Ellen M. Silva, Designed by Anna Shallman

0443 | Sea Urchin Hat, Contributed by Sarah Fay, Designed by topstitchgirl

0446 | Natural Earflap Hat, Contributed by ChezPlum, Designed by Sylvie Damey

0447 | Scala, Designed & Contributed by Woolly Wormhead

0445 | Scotty's Hat, Contributed by Thea Orozco, Designed by Nicole Lorenz

0444 | Stocking Cap, Designed & Contributed by Marie Segares, Underground Crafter

0448 | Blue Earflap Hat, Contributed by ChezPlum,
Designed by Sylvie Damey

0449 | Retro Stocking Cap, Designed
& Contributed by Margaret Hubert

0450 | Sloppy Joe, Designed &
Contributed by Woolly Wormhead

0453 | Arawn Celtic Knot, Designed &
Contributed by Katya Frankel

0452 | Cabled Pom-Pom Hat, Designed
& Contributed by Emily Simmons

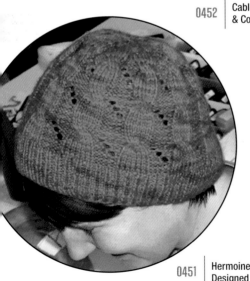

0451 | Hermoine Hat, Contributed by Sam Boice,
Designed by Lackie Lauseng

0454 | My So-Called Life Cabled Hat,
Designed & Contributed by Lee Meredith

0456 | MacDuff Hat, Designed & Contributed by Corrina Ferguson, PicnicKnits

0458 | Celtic Cable Cap, Contributed by Jill Packard, Designed by Jenna Wilson

0455 | Habitat, Contributed by Jill Packard, Designed by Jared Flood

0457 | Smocking Cap, Designed & Contributed by Brittany Wilson

0459 | Bob Newhart Cables Hat, Designed
& Contributed by Lee Meredith

0460 | Cabled Chemo Cap, Designed &
Contributed by Margit Sage of Fiber Fiend

0461 | OMG Hat, Contributed by the SWTC Collection,
Designed by Jonelle Raffino

0462 | Cable Brim Cap, Designed &
Contributed by Essie Woods Bruell

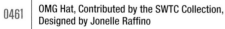

0465 | Uninspired Hat, Contributed by A.M., Designed by Stephanie Pearl-McPhee

0463 | Triple Knit Cable Hat, Designed & Contributed by Alasdair Post-Quinn

0464 | Smocking Cap, Designed & Contributed by Brittany Wilson

0468   Mama Sock, Designed & Contributed by Agnes Maderich, Hats by Agnes

0469   Mixed Cable Cap, Designed & Contributed by Essie Woods Bruell

0466   Cable Hat Too, Designed & Contributed by Marci Blank

0467   Oak Bark Cabled Hat 2, Designed & Contributed by Margit Sage of Fiber Fiend

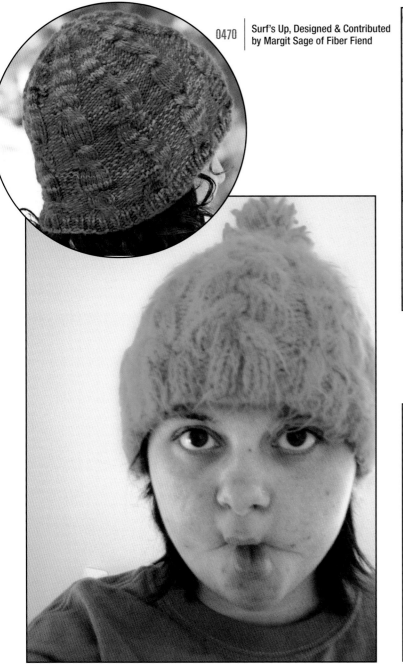

0470 | Surf's Up, Designed & Contributed by Margit Sage of Fiber Fiend

0472 | Ball Cap, Designed & Contributed by Mary Anne Cutler

0471 | Braided Hat, Contributed by Jasmine Davis, Designed by Anise

0473 | Mars Hat, Contributed by A. Greeley O'Connor, Designed by Véronik Avery

0475 | Braided Blue Beanie, Contributed by A.M.

0476 | Cable Hat, Designed & Contributed by Carolyn Vance

0474 | Kyla, Designed & Contributed by Katya Frankel

0477 | Turks Head, Contributed by A.M., Designed by Charlene Schurch

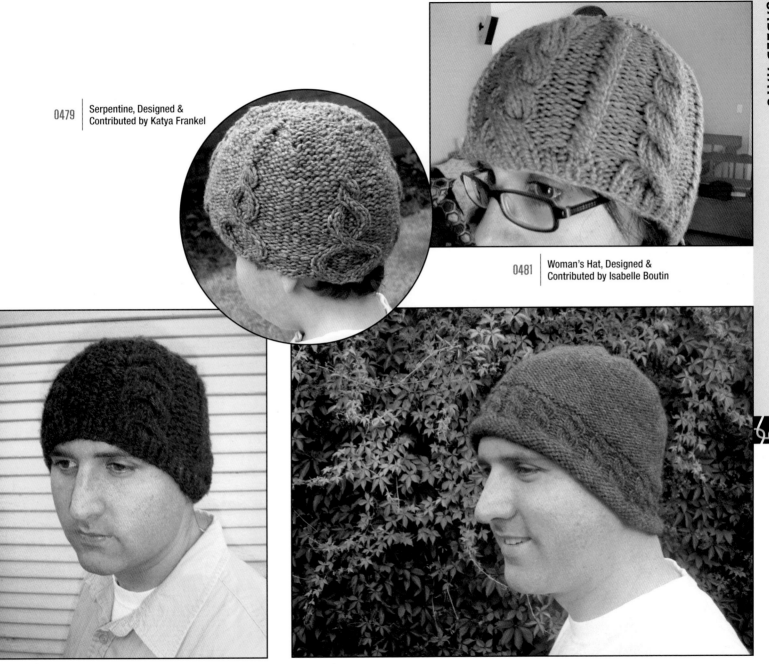

0479 | Serpentine, Designed & Contributed by Katya Frankel

0481 | Woman's Hat, Designed & Contributed by Isabelle Boutin

0478 | Chunky Double Cable, Designed & Contributed by Lois Ellen Designs

0480 | Inside-Out Cable Brim, Designed & Contributed by Lois Ellen Designs

0483   Shedir, Contributed by Anne Blayney,
Designed by Jenna Wilson

0484   Top Down Woman's Hat, Designed & Contributed
by Susan Dewey, Bee Berry Woods

0482   Elijah Hat, Designed &
Contributed by Diana Troldahl

0485   Wavelet Hat, Contributed by Agnes Maderich,
Hats by Agnes, Designed by Delicious Croissant

0487 | Noro Hat, Designed & Contributed by London Nelson

0486 | Cable Hat & Half Mittens, Designed & Contributed by AnneLena K. Mattison

0488 | Oak Bark Cabled Hat, Designed & Contributed by Margit Sage of Fiber Fiend

0490 | Knotty Cable Rimmed Beanie,
Designed & Contributed by Kim Helmick

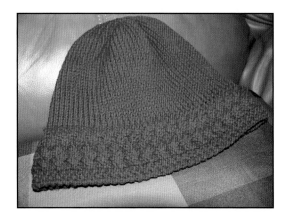

0491 | Short Row Aran Cap, Designed &
Contributed by Rebecca Harmon

0489 | Slip-Cable, Designed &
Contributed by Katya Frankel

0492 | Dulaan Scarf–Inspired Hat, Designed & Contributed by Rebecca Mercier

0495 | Fading Cables, Contributed by Jill Packard, Designed by Sarah Sturtevant

0493 | Woman's Hat, Contributed by Dana K. Smith, Designed by Christine Quirion

0494 | Surrey Hat, Designed & Contributed by Corrina Ferguson, PicnicKnits

0496 | Clamber, Designed & Contributed by
Laura Martos of Dizzy Blonde Studios

0497 | Binary Cables, Contributed by
Anne Blayney, Designed by Firefairy

0499 | Snarky Cables Hat,
Designed & Contributed by
Stephanie Goodwin-Ritter

0498 | Cables and Bobbles Beret, Contributed by
Alexandra Johnson, Designed by Marilyn Losee

0501 | Ligneous Cable Hat, Designed & Contributed by Elizabeth Carls

0500 | Tan Cabled Hat, Designed & Contributed by Rachel "Ivy" Clarke

0502 | Coronet, Contributed by Emily Simmons, Designed by Alexandra Virgiel

0506 | Marseille, Contributed by Jane Nowakowski, Designed by Denise Black / Sandy Scoville

0503 | Crocheted Bowler, Contributed by Louise Gordon, Designed by Kay Ribbens

0504 | Crochet Crusher Hat, Contributed by Jane Nowakowski, Designed by Evelyn A. Clark

0505 | Eleanor, Contributed by Rebecca Patterson, Designed by Linda Lanese for Artisan Yarns

0508 | Crocheted Beret, Designed
& Contributed by Louise Gordon

0507 | Woman's Hat, Designed & Contributed by
Josi Hannon Madera, Art of Crochet

0509 | Red Crochet Hat with Veil, Designed
& Contributed by Christina Marie Potter

0512 | Julie, Contributed by Rebecca Patterson, Designed by Linda Lanese for Artisan Yarns

0510 | Crocheted Feathered, Contributed by Louise Gordon, Designed by Kay Ribbens

0511 | Purple Outback, Designed & Contributed by Pam Pryshepa Ronan

0513 | Pink Bucket, Contributed by Maria Maxwell, Designed by Kay Ribbens

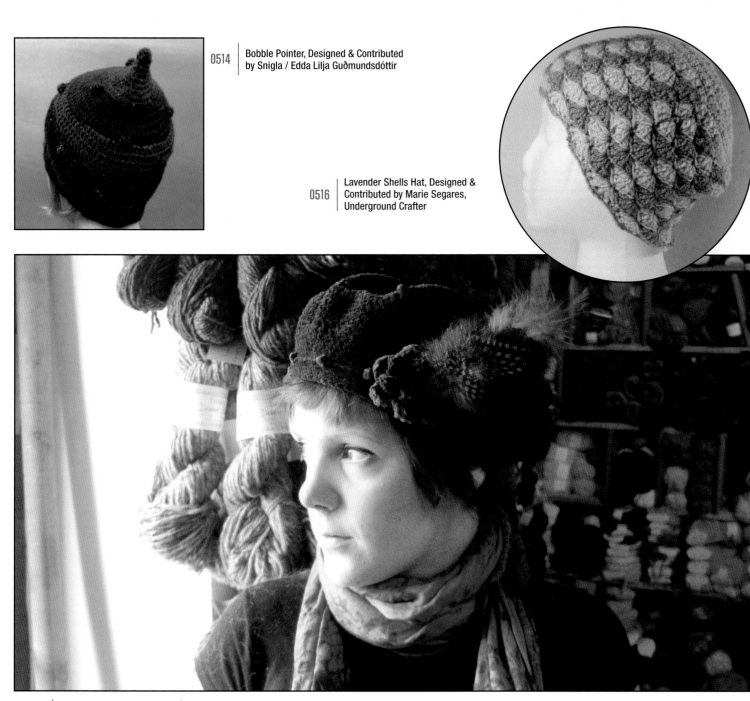

0514 | Bobble Pointer, Designed & Contributed by Snigla / Edda Lilja Guðmundsdóttir

0516 | Lavender Shells Hat, Designed & Contributed by Marie Segares, Underground Crafter

0515 | Raspberry Beret, Contributed by Louise Gordon, Designed by Kay Ribbens

0517 | Pink Rounder, Contributed by Maria Maxwell, Designed by Kay Ribbens

0519 | Rose Glow Cap, Designed & Contributed by Rebecca Harmon

0518 | Altay Purple, Contributed by ChezPlum, Designed by Sylvie Damey

0520 | Isabella, Contributed by Rebecca Patterson, Designed by Linda Lanese for Artisan Yarns

Crocheted Bucket, Contributed by
Louise Gordon, Designed by Kay Ribbens

0523 | Super Bulky Hat, Designed &
Contributed by Margaret Hubert

0522 | Altay Hat, Contributed by ChezPlum,
Designed by Sylvie Damey

0527 | Moss Suede Shells Hat, Designed & Contributed by Marie Segares, Underground Crafter

0524 | Yellow Beret, Contributed by Louise Gordon, Designed by Kay Ribbens

0525 | Chenille Cloche, Designed & Contributed by Margaret Hubert

0526 | Beret, Contributed by Maria Maxwell, Designed by Kay Ribbens

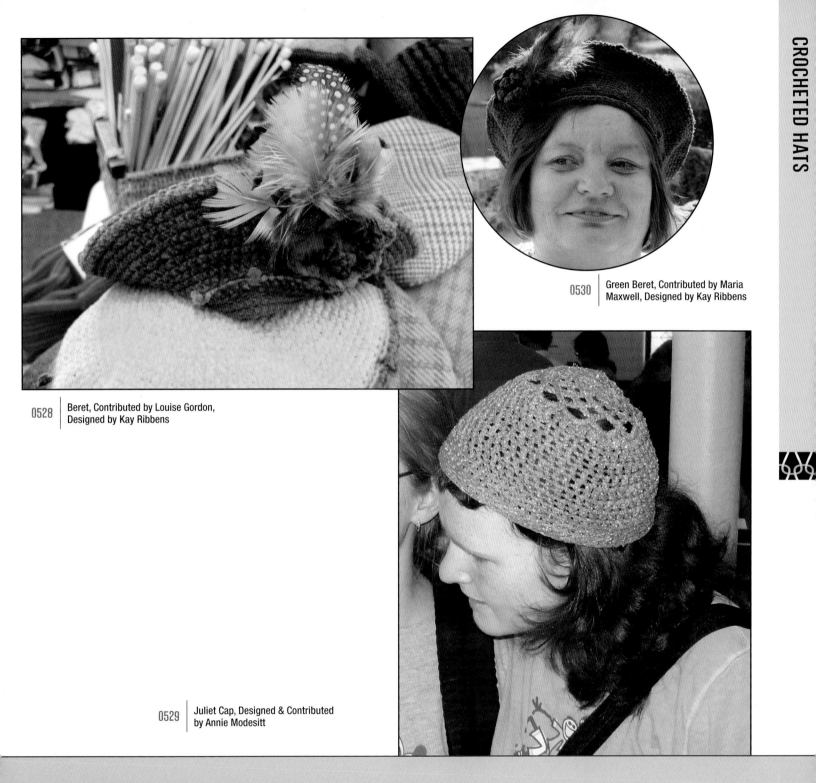

0530 | Green Beret, Contributed by Maria Maxwell, Designed by Kay Ribbens

0528 | Beret, Contributed by Louise Gordon, Designed by Kay Ribbens

0529 | Juliet Cap, Designed & Contributed by Annie Modesitt

0531 | Chenille Bucket, Designed & Contributed by Lynn Johanna, Lady Willow Designs
Photo by LadyWillow

0532 | Chenille Bonnet, Designed & Contributed by Lynn Johanna, Lady Willow Designs
Photo by LadyWillow

0533 | Woman's Hat, Designed & Contributed by Josi Hannon Madera, Art of Crochet

0535 | Brown Flower Cloche, Designed & Contributed by Snigla / Edda Lilja Guðmundsdóttir

0536 | Chenille Visor, Designed & Contributed by Lynn Johanna, Lady Willow Designs
Photo by LadyWillow

0534 | Unisex Hat, Designed & Contributed by Josi Hannon Madera, Art of Crochet

0537 | Chenille Helmet, Designed & Contributed by Lynn Johanna, Lady Willow Designs
Photo by LadyWillow

0541 | Banana Leaf Hat, Designed & Contributed by Kathy North

0538 | Kick the Bucket, Contributed by Marie Stanley, That 80's Hat

0539 | Crochet Crusher Hat, Contributed by Jane Nowakowski, Designed by Evelyn A. Clark

0540 | Pink Bowler, Contributed by Louise Gordon, Designed by Kay Ribbens

0543 | Madison Ave., Contributed by Jane Nowakowski, Designed by Denise Black / Sandy Scoville

0544 | Peruvian Hat, Designed & Contributed by Margaret Hubert

0542 | Denver, Contributed by Jane Nowakowski, Designed by Denise Black / Sandy Scoville

0545 | Two-Toned Hat, Designed & Contributed by Annette M. Davis-Dill

0548 | Brown Flower Cloche,
Designed & Contributed by Snigla /
Edda Lilja Guðmundsdóttir

0547 | Post Stitch Hat with Brim, Designed
& Contributed by Marie Segares,
Underground Crafter

0546 | Chunky Shells Hat, Designed &
Contributed by Marie Segares,
Underground Crafter

0549 | Passerby MK Hat 3, Contributed by
Jane Nowakowski, Designed by SM Kahn

0551 | Striped Beret,
Contributed by Maria Maxwell

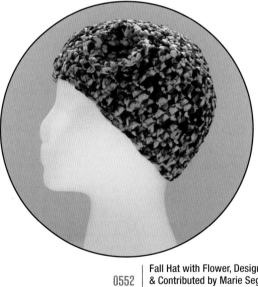

0552 | Fall Hat with Flower, Designed
& Contributed by Marie Segares,
Underground Crafter

0550 | Chenille Cloche, Designed & Contributed
by Lynn Johanna, Lady Willow Designs

Photo by LadyWillow

0554 | Ester, Contributed by
Rebecca Patterson, Designed by
Linda Lanese for Artisan Yarns

0555 | Purple Beret, Contributed by Maria Maxwell,
Designed by Kay Ribbens

0556 | Open Round,
Contributed by Maria Maxwell

0553 | Changing Moods Hat, Designed & Contributed by
Lynn Johanna, Lady Willow Designs

Photo by LadyWillow

0558 | Diana, Contributed by Rebecca Patterson, Designed by Linda Lanese for Artisan Yarns

0559 | Woman's Beret, Designed & Contributed by Jane Nowakowski

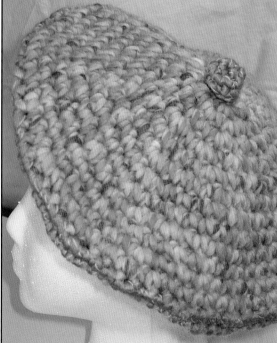

0557 | Kelly, Contributed by Rebecca Patterson, Designed by Linda Lanese for Artisan Yarns

0560 | On Broadway, Contributed by Jane Nowakowski, Designed by Denise Black / Sandy Scoville

0562 | Peach Cooler, Designed & Contributed by Margaret Hubert

0561 | Muster Cap, Designed & Contributed by Pam Pryshepa Ronan

0563 | Mesh Cap, Designed & Contributed by Margaret Hubert

0565 | Starburst, Contributed by Yvonne Allen, Designed by Woolly Wormhead

0564 | Arch Rival, Designed & Contributed by Becca Robbins

0566 | Aqua Claudia, Designed & Contributed by Becca Robbins

0568 | Floppy Brim Hat,
Contributed by Lisa Janowsky,
Designed by Linda Cyr Rounds

0569 | Alseid Hat, Designed & Contributed by
Corrina Ferguson, PicnicKnits

0570 | Kerchief, Contributed by Rebecca Mercier,
Designed by Magistra Lanam Amat

0567 | Tudor Cap 2, Contributed by Yvonne Allen,
Designed by Woolly Wormhead

0572 | Charity Lace Cable Watch, Designed & Contributed by Tricia Fagley, random threads designs

0573 | Backyard Leaves Hat, Designed & Contributed by Rebecca Mercier

0571 | Enroule, Contributed by Patricia Would, Cottonon, Designed by Woolly Wormhead

0574 | Crumpet Beret, Contributed by Constance M. Cole, Designed by Maura Kirk

0576 | Knit Winter Hat, Designed & Contributed by Mary Anne Cutler

0577 | Black White Millinery, Designed & Contributed by Annie Modesitt

0575 | Superior Lace Veil, Designed & Contributed by Annie Modesitt

0578 | Trellis Beret, Designed & Contributed by Woolly Wormhead

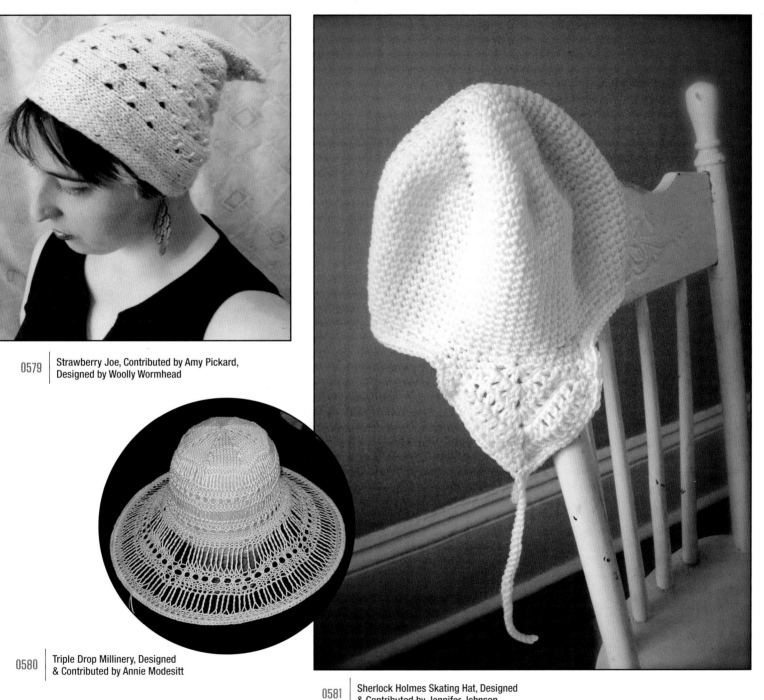

0579 | Strawberry Joe, Contributed by Amy Pickard,
Designed by Woolly Wormhead

0580 | Triple Drop Millinery, Designed
& Contributed by Annie Modesitt

0581 | Sherlock Holmes Skating Hat, Designed
& Contributed by Jennifer Johnson

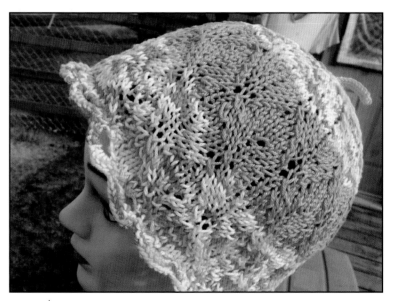

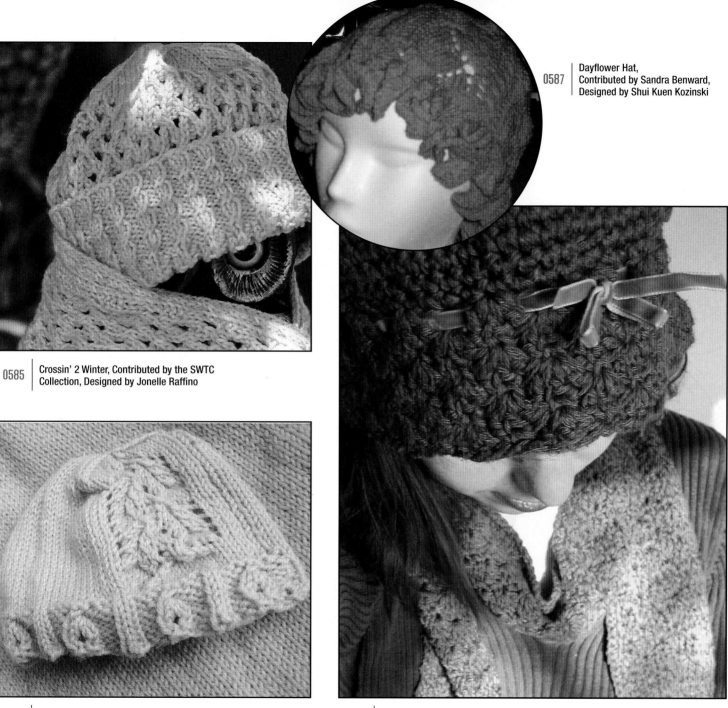

0587 | Dayflower Hat,
Contributed by Sandra Benward,
Designed by Shui Kuen Kozinski

0585 | Crossin' 2 Winter, Contributed by the SWTC
Collection, Designed by Jonelle Raffino

0586 | Pea Pod Baby Hat / Set, Contributed
by Anne Blayney, Designed by Kate Gilbert

0588 | The Brittnay Hat, Designed & Contributed by
Katie Harmon, PinkPolish Design

0590 OneGora, Designed & Contributed by Lisa Putnam

0591 Spectator Grand, Contributed by Lisa Janowsky, Designed by Annie Modesitt

0589 Crocheted Floral Cap, Designed & Contributed by Kelly Klem of Klymyshyn Design

0592 Black Millinery, Designed & Contributed by Annie Modesitt

0594 | Lace Pith, Designed & Contributed by
Annie Modesitt

0595 | Lady's Beret, Contributed
by Patricia Would, Cottonon,
Designed by Woolly Wormhead

0593 | Aster Tam, Designed &
Contributed by Kendra Nitta

0598 Pink Triple Drop, Designed & Contributed by Annie Modesitt

0597 A Cap for Eva, Designed & Contributed by Catherine Henry

0596 Bad Hair Day Hat, Contributed by Agnes Maderich, Hats by Agnes, Designed by Chrissy Gardiner

0599 Striped Beret, Contributed by Patricia Would, Cottonon, Designed by Woolly Wormhead

0600 | Foliage Hat, Contributed by Anne Blayney,
Designed by Emilee Mooney

0601 | Lace Beret, Contributed by Amy Pickard,
Designed by Woolly Wormhead

0602 | Lace Cloche, Designed & Contributed
by Annie Modesitt

0603 | Starburst, Designed & Contributed
by Woolly Wormhead

0604 | Hairpin Hat, Designed & Contributed by Dana Lorz

0606 | Foliage, Contributed by Jessica Cheney, Designed by Emilee Mooney

0605 | Spin Me Right 'Round, Baby, Contributed by Jessica Cheney, Designed by Solveig Engevold

0607 | Buffalo Gold Wimple, Designed & Contributed by Annie Modesitt

0609 | Windward, Contributed by Patricia Would, Cottonon, Designed by Woolly Wormhead

0608 | Bad Hair Day Hat, Contributed by Agnes Maderich, Hats by Agnes, Designed by Chrissy Gardiner

0611 | Favorite Colors, Designed &
Contributed by Pam Pryshepa Ronan

0612 | Divine Hat, Contributed by Brenda Cunningham,
Designed by Rheatheylia

0610 | Women's Slouchy Hat with Brim, Designed &
Contributed by Tabitha Dick Oyediran, Knits So Divine

0613 | Women's Slouchy Beret, Designed & Contributed
by Tabitha Dick Oyediran, Knits So Divine

0616 | Frillby, Contributed by Pam Pryshepa Ronan, Designed by Drew Emborsky

0615 | Odessa, Contributed by Anne Crawford, Designed by Grumperina

0614 | Leaf Pattern Hat, Designed & Contributed by Tabitha Dick Oyediran, Knits So Divine

0617 | Meret, Contributed by Patricia Would, Cottonon, Designed by Woolly Wormhead

0618 | Rainbow Hat, Contributed by Toni Blye,
Designed by It's Curious

0621 | Sweet Georgia, Designed
& Contributed by Brittany Wilson

0619 | Vintage Auto Bonnet, Designed &
Contributed by Pam Pryshepa Ronan

0620 | Floppy Fall Beret, Designed &
Contributed by Rebecca Velasquez

0622 | Trellis Beret, Contributed by Constance M. Cole,
Designed by Woolly Wormhead

0623 | May Flowers Hat, Contributed by Toni Blye,
Designed by It's Curious

0624 | Sweet Georgia, Designed &
Contributed by Brittany Wilson

0626 | Lady's Beret, Contributed by Patricia Would,
Cottonon, Designed by Woolly Wormhead

0625 | My So-Called Life Lace Hat,
Designed & Contributed by Lee Meredith

0627 | Ziggy, Designed &
Contributed by Woolly Wormhead

0630 | Clapotis-Inspired Hat,
Contributed by Rebecca
Mercier (inspired by Kate
Gilbert's "Clapotis"), Designed
by Needles & Hooks

0628 | Springtime in Philadelphia Beret, Contributed by
Constance M. Cole, Designed by Kate Gagnon

0629 | Rhapsody Hat, Designed &
Contributed by Terry Liann Morris

0631 | Swirl, Designed &
Contributed by Dana Lorz

0633 | Trellis Beret, Contributed by Patricia Would, Cottonon, Designed by Woolly Wormhead

0635 | Leaf Hat, Designed & Contributed by Rebecca Mercier

0634 | Lacy Head Wrap, Designed & Contributed by Sharon Menges

0632 | Foliage, Designed & Contributed by Stephanie Goodwin-Ritter

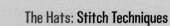

0638 | Lace Band Hat, Designed &
Contributed by Ruth Altheim

0636 | Simple Head Wrap, Designed &
Contributed by Sharon Menges

0637 | Squash Blossom, Contributed by Snigla
/ Edda Lilja Guðmundsdóttir

0639 | Rose Red, Contributed by Yvonne Allen,
Designed by Ysolda Teague

0643 | Virginia Cloche, Designed & Contributed by Annie Modesitt

0641 | Scala, Contributed by Yvonne Allen, Designed by Woolly Wormhead

0640 | Blue Twinkle, Designed & Contributed by Pam Pryshepa Ronan

0642 | Lace Wrap Hat, Designed & Contributed by Rebecca Mercier

0645 | Gatsby, Contributed by the SWTC Collection, Designed by Amy Polcyn

0644 | Vintage Sunlight Hat, Designed & Contributed by Pam Pryshepa Ronan

0646 | Daisy, Contributed by Patricia Would, Cottonon, Designed by Woolly Wormhead

0648 | Fascinator, Designed & Contributed by Pam Pryshepa Ronan

0650 | Cranberry Adult Petal Hat, Designed & Contributed by Katie Harmon, PinkPolish Design

0647 | Spectator Grand Hat, Contributed by Marina Hayes, Designed by Annie Modesitt

0649 | Lace Woman's Hat, Designed & Contributed by Shannita Williams-Alleyne

0651 | Zinnia Tam, Designed & Contributed by Rebecca Harmon

0652 | Blue & Pink Hat, Designed & Contributed by Lorraine Ehrlinger Designs

0653 | Rosebuds Felted Hat, Designed & Contributed by Rebecca Harmon

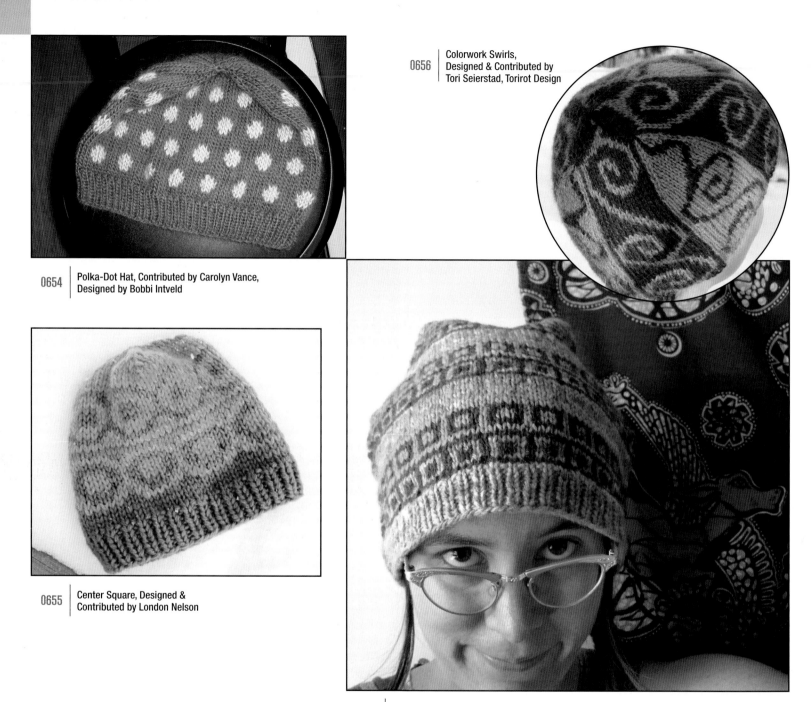

0654 | Polka-Dot Hat, Contributed by Carolyn Vance, Designed by Bobbi Intveld

0656 | Colorwork Swirls, Designed & Contributed by Tori Seierstad, Torirot Design

0655 | Center Square, Designed & Contributed by London Nelson

0657 | Squares Squared Hat, Designed & Contributed by Cosette Cornelius-Bates

0659 | Fairbanks Hat, Designed &
Contributed by Cosette Cornelius-Bates

0658 | Selbu Modern, Contributed by Sarah Fay,
Designed by Kate Gagnon

0660 | Check Mate Hat, Designed & Contributed by
Kelly Klem of Klymyshyn Design

The Hats: Stitch Techniques   201

0661 | Partial Colorwork Women's Hat, Designed & Contributed by Emily Simmons

0664 | Checkered Twined Hat, Contributed by Carolyn Vance, Designed by Anne Maj-Ling

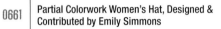

0662 | Bicolored Slouch, Designed & Contributed by Terry Liann Morris

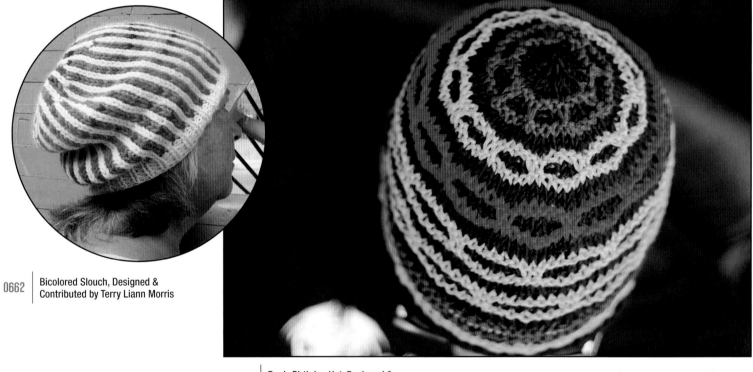

0663 | Ben's Birthday Hat, Designed & Contributed by Lee Meredith

0667 | Ocean Waves Cap, Designed & Contributed by Rebecca Harmon

0665 | Oh, Snap!, Contributed by Ellen M. Silva, Designed by Black Water Abbey

0666 | Bohus Inspiration, Designed & Contributed by Bohus, Knit by Bonnie Esplie

0668 | Nepali Hat, Designed & Contributed by Tina Whitmore for Knitwhits

0670 | Tam, Contributed by Margaret A. Martin,
Designed by Angela Sixian Wu

0669 | New Wave Colors, Designed &
Contributed by Terry Liann Morris

0671 | Diamond Hat, Designed & Contributed
by Tina Whitmore for Knitwhits

0674 | Crazy Colors Tam, Designed & Contributed by Rebecca Harmon

0672 | Manos Hat, Contributed by Tricia Fagley, Designed by Becky Graves

0673 | Acrylic Stranded, Designed & Contributed by Carolyn Vance

0675 | Stained Glass Felted Hat, Designed & Contributed by Rebecca Harmon

0677 | Rippling Waves Cap, Designed & Contributed by Rebecca Harmon

0676 | Woman's Toque with Colourwork Band, Contributed by Suzanne Carter-Jackson, Designed by Sweaterkits

0678 | 50 Villapeikkoa, Designed & Contributed by Stephanie Voyer

0681 | Vaguely Norwegian, Contributed by A.M.

0680 | Kaz Thrummed Hat, Designed & Contributed by Terry Liann Morris

0679 | Inga's Hat, Contributed by Carolyn Vance, Designed by Sheila MacDonald

0682 | Starry Sky Cap, Designed & Contributed by Rebecca Harmon

0684 | Woman's Colorwork Hat, Designed & Contributed by Carol Feller, Stolen Stitches

0685 | Fall Colors Felted Hat, Designed & Contributed by Rebecca Harmon

0683 | Spring Flowers Tam, Designed & Contributed by Rebecca Harmon

0687 | Red & White Heart Colorwork,
Contributed by Lies Spaink,
Designed by Anne Featonby

0688 | Falling Blocks Hat, Designed &
Contributed by Alasdair Post-Quinn

0686 | Autumn Swirl Cap, Designed &
Contributed by Rebecca Harmon

0689 | Argyle Hat, Designed &
Contributed by Carolyn Vance

0690 | Grey Domino Tam, Designed & Contributed by Rebecca Harmon

0691 | Red Beret, Designed & Contributed by Tricia Fagley

0692 | We Call Them Pirates, Contributed by Ellen M. Silva, Designed by Adrian Bizilia

0694 | Fake Isle Hat, Contributed by AnneLena K. Mattison, Designed by Amy King

0695 | Black & White Snowflake Hat, Contributed by Lies Spaink, Designed by Bea Ellis

0696 | Amalie's Hat, Designed & Contributed by AnneLena K. Mattison

0693 | Flowers in the Snow Reflection, Designed & Contributed by Cosette Cornelius-Bates

0699 | Groovy Colorwork,
Contributed by Sandra Benward

0697 | Falling Blocks Hat, Designed &
Contributed by Alasdair Post-Quinn

0698 | Brickwork Hat, Contributed by Sandra Benward,
Designed by Terry Liann Morris

0700 | Woman's Ski Hat, Designed & Contributed
by Josi Hannon Madera, Art of Crochet

0702 | Brickwork Hat, Designed &
Contributed by Terry Liann Morris

0701 | Fiber Fiesta, Contributed by Celeste Nossiter,
Designed by Ruth Sorensen

0703 | Ski Hat, Designed &
Contributed by Margaret Hubert

0705 | Green White Hat, Designed & Contributed by Carolyn Vance

0706 | Unisex Hat, Designed & Contributed by Josi Hannon Madera, Art of Crochet

0704 | Raj, Designed & Contributed by Tori Seierstad, Torirot Design

0709 | Fair Isle Simple Hat, Contributed by Tricia Fagley, Designed by Amy Detjen

0708 | Colorwork Hat, Designed & Contributed by Annie Modesitt

0707 | Old-Fashioned Watch Cap, Contributed by Toni Blye, Designed by It's Curious

0710 | Pippi Blue, Designed & Contributed by Michele Lee Bernstein, PDXKnitterati

0711 | Kortelopet, Designed &
Contributed by Rebecca Ganzel

0713 | Hand-Dyed Wool Cap, Contributed by
Lorna Miser, Designed by Mike Wren

0712 | Spot Hat, Designed & Contributed
by Lois Ellen Designs

0714 | Snowflake Hat, Designed & Contributed by Katie
Harmon, PinkPolish Design

0717 | Fair Isle Stash Hat, Designed & Contributed by Carolyn Vance

0715 | Glengarry, Contributed by Rachel Kluesner, Designed by Vicki Square
Photo by Sungazing Photography

0716 | Arrrgyle Skulls, Designed & Contributed by Anne Kuo Lukito

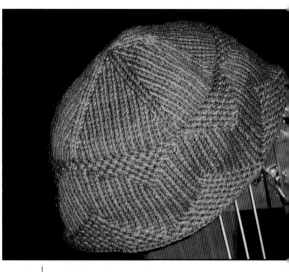

0720 | Purple Twined Hat, Designed & Contributed by Carolyn Vance

0718 | EZ Stash Hat, Contributed by Carolyn Vance, Designed by Elizabeth Zimmerman

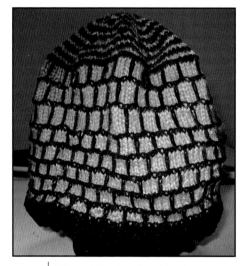

0719 | Brickwork Hat, Contributed by Lisa Stanton, Designed by Terry Liann Morris

0721 | Patrick's Felted Twined Fair Isle, Designed & Contributed by Carolyn Vance

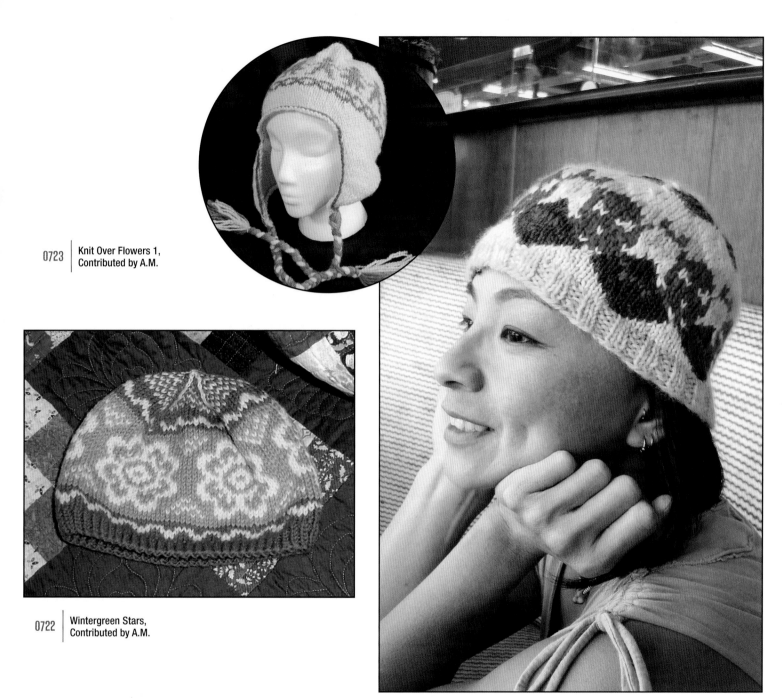

0723 | Knit Over Flowers 1,
Contributed by A.M.

0722 | Wintergreen Stars,
Contributed by A.M.

0724 | Arrrgyle Skulls, Designed & Contributed
by Anne Kuo Lukito

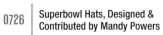

0726 | Superbowl Hats, Designed & Contributed by Mandy Powers

0727 | Pippi Earflap Hat, Designed & Contributed by Michele Lee Bernstein, PDXKnitterati

0725 | Tamberet, Contributed by Rachel Kluesner, Designed by Dyeabolical Yarns

Photo by Sungazing Photography

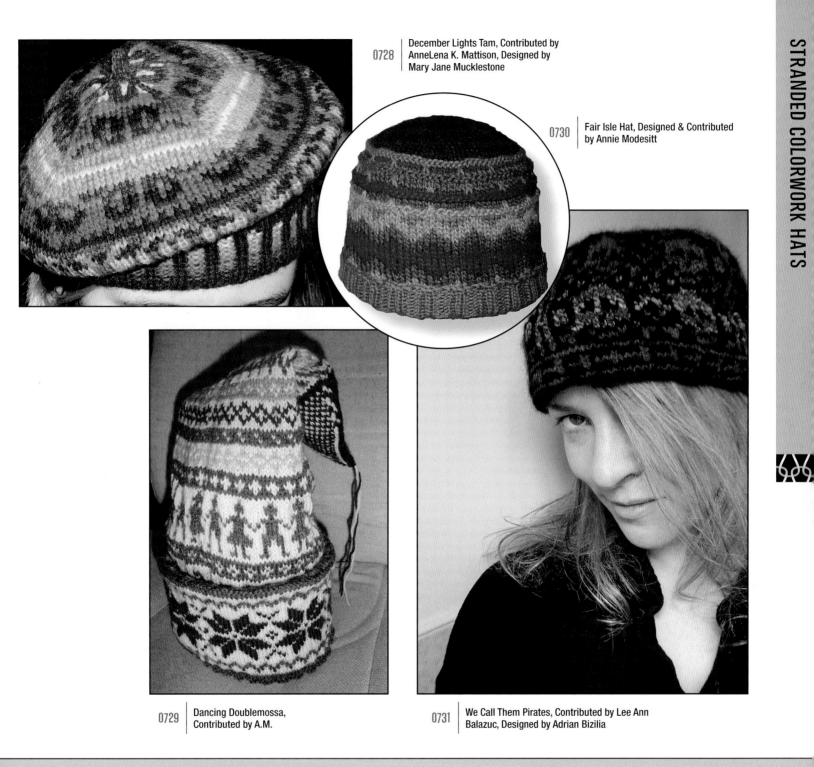

0728 | December Lights Tam, Contributed by AnneLena K. Mattison, Designed by Mary Jane Mucklestone

0730 | Fair Isle Hat, Designed & Contributed by Annie Modesitt

0729 | Dancing Doublemossa, Contributed by A.M.

0731 | We Call Them Pirates, Contributed by Lee Ann Balazuc, Designed by Adrian Bizilia

0733 | Dulcie, Contributed by Patricia Would,
Cottonon, Designed by Woolly Wormhead

0734 | A Touch of Whimsey, Designed &
Contributed by Rebecca Mercier

0732 | Spiral Hat, Designed &
Contributed by Marci Blank

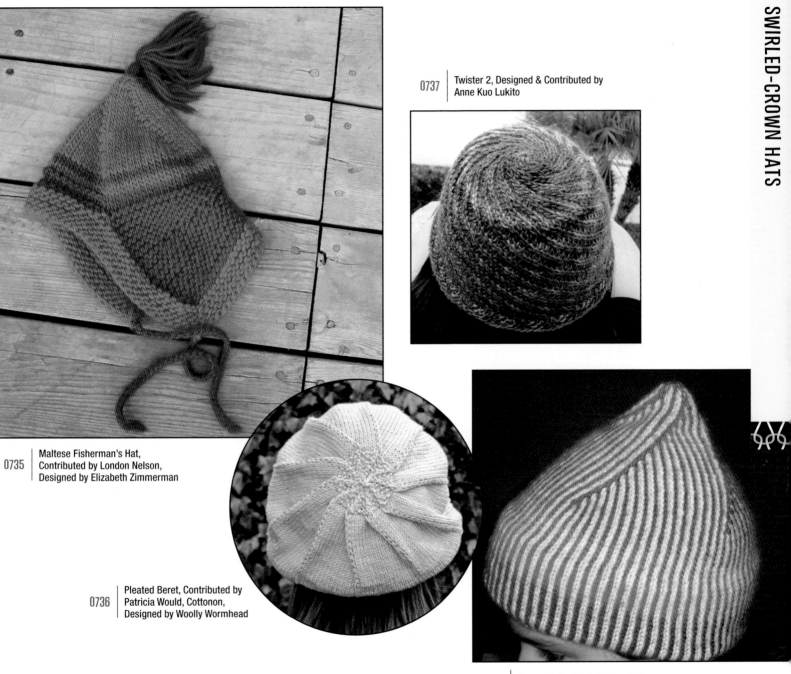

0737 | Twister 2, Designed & Contributed by Anne Kuo Lukito

0735 | Maltese Fisherman's Hat, Contributed by London Nelson, Designed by Elizabeth Zimmerman

0736 | Pleated Beret, Contributed by Patricia Would, Cottonon, Designed by Woolly Wormhead

0738 | Poems Twined Hat, Designed & Contributed by Carolyn Vance

0740 | Twined Mirasol Hat, Designed & Contributed by Carolyn Vance

0741 | Diamonds Tam, Designed & Contributed by Rebecca Harmon

0739 | Coldharbour Twist, Contributed by Yvonne Allen, Designed by Woolly Wormhead

0742 | Colorwork Hat, Designed & Contributed by Carla Hukee

0745 | Stella's Flat-Top Hat, Designed & Contributed by Melissa LaBarre

0743 | Holiday Odessa, Contributed by Brittany Wilson, Designed by Grumperina

0744 | Jamaican Tamberet, Designed & Contributed by Helen Jacobs-Grant

Photo by Lionel Jacobs

0746 | Slouchy Orange Hat, Designed & Contributed by Melissa LaBarre

0748 | Twister 1, Designed &
Contributed by Anne Kuo Lukito

0747 | Piedmont Slouch Hat,
Designed & Contributed by Sarah E. Sipe

0749 | Twister 2, Designed &
Contributed by Anne Kuo Lukito

0750 | Star of the Day, Contributed by Jill Packard,
Designed by Susan Lawrence

0753 | Man's Alpaca Hat, Designed &
Contributed by Anne Blayney

0751 | Wedge Hat, Designed & Contributed
by Charisa Martin Cairn

0752 | Frog Hat, Designed & Contributed
by Suzanne Carter-Jackson

0755 | Kipah, Designed &
Contributed by Joanne Seiff

0757 | Triple-Knit Hat, Designed &
Contributed by Alasdair Post-Quinn

0754 | Embossed Leaf Beret, Designed
& Contributed by Amy McElwain

0756 | Unspun Hat, Contributed by Rachel Kluesner,
Designed by Dyeabolical Yarns

Photo by Sungazing Photography

0761 | Celtic Banners Hat, Designed & Contributed by Alasdair Post-Quinn

0759 | Seaman's Cap, Contributed by Suzanne Carter-Jackson, Designed by Brenda Zuk

0758 | Woman's Hat, Designed & Contributed by Josi Hannon Madera, Art of Crochet

0760 | Handspun Snail Hat, Contributed by Cosette Cornelius-Bates, Designed by Elizabeth Zimmerman

0763 | Woman's Hat, Designed &
Contributed by Zoë Valette

0764 | Beret, Contributed by Anne Crawford,
Designed by Louisa Harding

0765 | Bobbled Cabled Chemo Cap, Designed &
Contributed by Margit Sage of Fiber Fiend

0762 | Threesome, Designed &
Contributed by Anne Kuo Lukito

0767 | Reverie Beret,
Contributed by Constance M. Cole,
Designed by Amy Swenson

0766 | Stars & Stripes Hat, Designed &
Contributed by Lorraine Ehrlinger Designs

0768 | Spin Me 'Round, Contributed by Anne Crawford,
Designed by Solveig Engevold

0769 | Sk8in Tamberet, Designed & Contributed by Helen Jacobs-Grant

Photo by Lionel Jacobs

0771 | Acorn Bobble Hat, Designed & Contributed by Kathy North

0770 | Akkol Hat, Designed & Contributed by Terry Liann Morris

0772 | Threesome Altered, Designed
& Contributed by Anne Kuo Lukito

0774 | Threesome Again, Designed &
Contributed by Anne Kuo Lukito

0773 | Spiral Rib Cap, Designed & Contributed by Michele
Lee Bernstein, PDXKnitterati

0775 | Indio Hat, Designed & Contributed
by Tina Whitmore for Knitwhits

0776 | Dulcie, Contributed by Patricia Would, Cottonon,
Designed by Woolly Wormhead

0778 | Women's Slouchy Hat, Designed & Contributed
by Tabitha Dick Oyediran, Knits So Divine

0779 | Three-Spiral Hat, Contributed by Mandy Powers, Designed by Elizabeth Zimmerman

0780 | Frosty Morning, Designed & Contributed by Agnes Maderich, Hats by Agnes

0781 | Pillbox Confection, Designed & Contributed by Sharon Hanson

0782 | Bobble Beret, Designed & Contributed by Joelle Burbank, Adirondack Knits

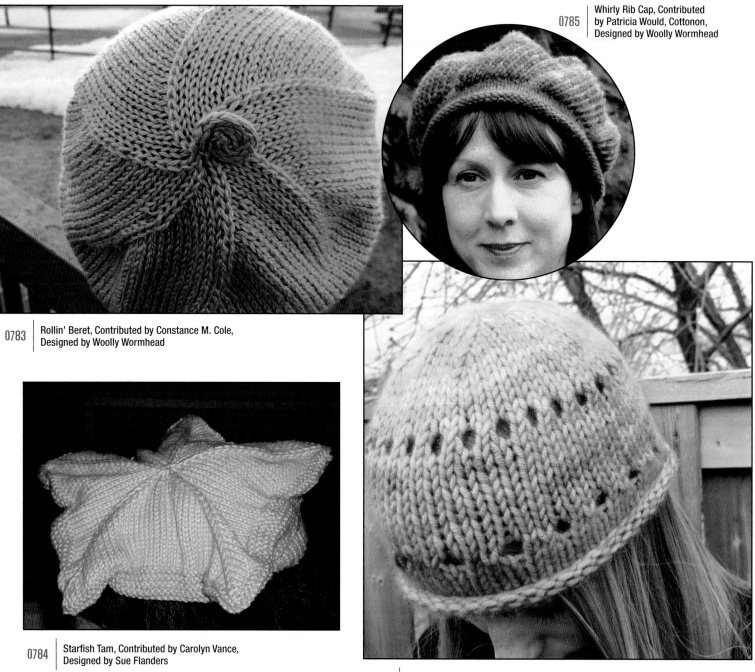

0783 | Rollin' Beret, Contributed by Constance M. Cole, Designed by Woolly Wormhead

0784 | Starfish Tam, Contributed by Carolyn Vance, Designed by Sue Flanders

0786 | Cashmere Eyelet Hat, Designed & Contributed by Emily Simmons

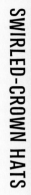

0788 | Marble Muffin, Contributed by Yvonne Allen, Designed by Woolly Wormhead

0789 | Sea Swirl Ribbed Cap, Designed & Contributed by Rebecca Harmon

0790 | Baby Pixie Hat,
Contributed by Mandy Furney

0791 | Tea Cozy Hat, Designed & Contributed
by Louise Gordon

0792 | Jester Hat, Designed & Contributed
by Tina Whitmore for Knitwhits

0793 | Good Day Sunshine Hat, Designed & Contributed by Janel Laidman

0795 | Wiggly Stripes, Designed & Contributed by Edie Eckman

0794 | Charity Child, Designed & Contributed by Lizette Hopkins

0796 | Spiral Hat, Contributed by Maria Hanson, Designed by Nancy Delcomyn

0797 | Ribbons and Bows, Designed & Contributed by Debby Ware

0798 | Lace Dahlia, Designed & Contributed by Jennifer J. Cirka, Jaybird Designs
Photo by Robin Long Photography

0799 | Lavender with Buds, Contributed by Michelle Tibbs & Elizabeth Cadieux

0800 | Kilkenny, Designed & Contributed by Woolly Wormhead

0801 | Bell Ruffle Toddler Hat, Designed & Contributed by Kathy North

0803 | Doodle, Designed & Contributed by Woolly Wormhead

0802 | Porcupine, Designed & Contributed by Woolly Wormhead

0804 | Butterfly Trail Cap, Contributed by Tot Toppers, Designed by Kathryn L. Oates

Photo by KSC Photography

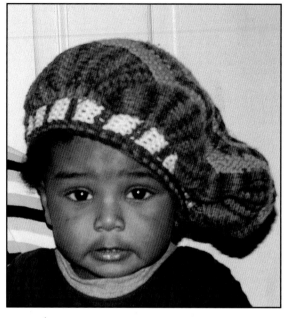

0806 | Safari Tamberet, Designed &
Contributed by Helen Jacobs-Grant

Photo by Lionel Jacobs

0805 | Pumpkin Hats, Designed &
Contributed by Marina Hayes

0807 | Orange Thin Stripes, Contributed by
Michelle Tibbs & Elizabeth Cadieux

0809 | Propeller Hat,
Contributed by Yvonne Allen,
Designed by Woolly Wormhead

0808 | Pumpkin Beret,
Designed & Contributed by
Jessie J. Peissig

0810 | Purple Orange Stripe, Contributed by
Michelle Tibbs & Elizabeth Cadieux

0811 | Propeller, Designed &
Contributed by Woolly Wormhead

0813 | Baby Cables, Designed & Contributed by Edie Eckman

0814 | Striped Toddler's Hat, Designed & Contributed by Carol Feller, Stolen Stitches

0812 | Inside-Out Chunky Stocking, Contributed by Tot Toppers, Designed by Kathryn L. Oates

Photo by KSC Photography

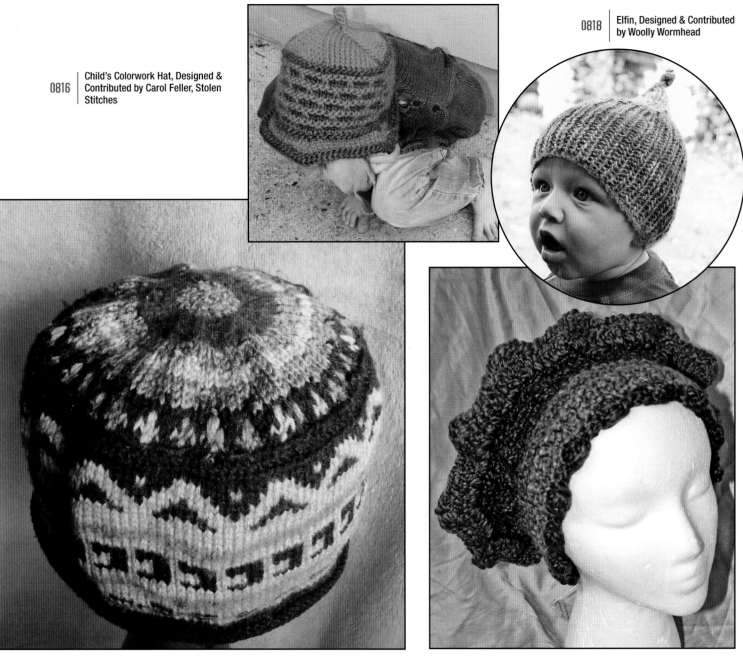

0816 | Child's Colorwork Hat, Designed & Contributed by Carol Feller, Stolen Stitches

0818 | Elfin, Designed & Contributed by Woolly Wormhead

0815 | Child's Intasia Hat, Designed & Contributed by Anne E. P. Boyer

0817 | Waves Head Wrap, Designed & Contributed by Sharon Menges

0819 | Preemie Hat, Designed &
Contributed by Jane Nowakowski

0820 | Squash Blossom, Designed & Contributed
by Snigla / Edda Lilja Guðmundsdóttir

0821 | Sophia's First Hat, Designed &
Contributed by Sophia Raffino

0823 | Orange Cutie Hat, Contributed by Sue Caldwell,
Lovely Yarns, Designed by Debbie Ware

0824 | Gold, Red Cloche, Designed & Contributed
by Snigla / Edda Lilja Guðmundsdóttir

0825 | Flowers and Fluff, Designed &
Contributed by Debby Ware

0827 | Rosebuds Band, Contributed by
Michelle Tibbs & Elizabeth Cadieux

0826 | Fuzzy Bunny Hat, Designed & Contributed by
Katie Harmon, PinkPolish Design

0828 | Flower Brimmed Child's Hat, Designed & Contributed
by Kelly Klem, Klymyshyn Design

0830 | Sale Hat, Designed &
Contributed by Cynthia Marovich

0831 | Baby I-Cord Beany, Designed &
Contributed by Woolly Wormhead

0829 | Hat with Rosette, Designed & Contributed by
Jennifer J. Cirka, Jaybird Designs
Photo by Robin Long Photography

0832 | Pink Ribbons, Contributed by
Michelle Tibbs & Elizabeth Cadieux

0834 | Brain Hat, Contributed by the SWTC Collection, Designed by Jonelle Raffino

0833 | Buzzbee, Designed & Contributed by Woolly Wormhead

0835 | Petal Hat, Designed & Contributed by Katie Harmon, PinkPolish Design

0837 | Flat Hat, Designed & Contributed by Michelle Kennedy

0838 | Baby Sock, Designed & Contributed by Agnes Maderich, Hats by Agnes

0836 | Blue Onion Hat, Designed & Contributed by Katie Harmon, PinkPolish Design

0839 | Waltzer, Designed & Contributed by Woolly Wormhead

0843 | Zoe's Baby Hat, Designed & Contributed by Cheryl Shores

0841 | Bunny Hat, Designed & Contributed by Lorna Miser

0842 | Bobble Beret, Designed & Contributed by Michelle Kennedy

0840 | Crocheted Child's Sun Bonnet, Designed & Contributed by Kelly Klem of Klymyshyn Design

0846 | One-Skein Baby Hat,
Contributed by Angela Tong,
Designed by Leigh Radford

0844 | Baby Bonnet, Contributed by Louise
Gordon

0845 | Bluebell Flower Hat, Designed & Contributed by
Michelle Kennedy

0848 | Mix Hat, Contributed by ChezPlum, Designed by Sylvie Damey

0850 | Striped Pom-Pom, Designed & Contributed by Snigla / Edda Lilja Guðmundsdóttir

0847 | Newborn Pixie Hat, Contributed by Alexandra Johnson, Designed by Natalie B

0849 | Preemie Easter Hat, Contributed by Tricia Fagley, Designed by Chell

0852 | Antenna Hat, Designed & Contributed by Essie Woods Bruell

0851 | Coney Baby Hat, Contributed by Angela Tong, Designed by Vyvyan Neel

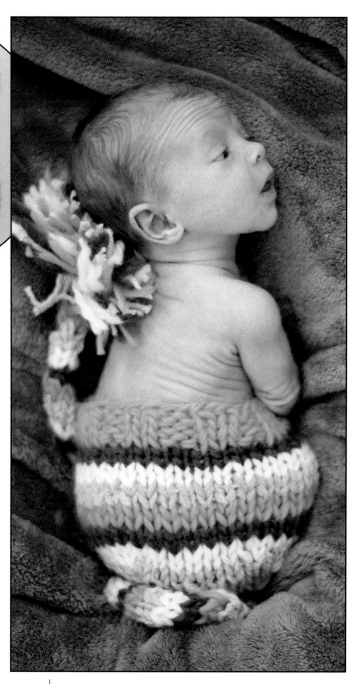

0853 | Chunky Striped Stocking, Contributed by Tot Toppers, Designed by Kathryn L. Oates

Photo by KSC Photography

0855   Dots and Ruffles, Designed & Contributed by Debby Ware

0857   Preppy Baby, Contributed by Michelle Tibbs & Elizabeth Cadieux

0856   Ribbon Hat, Contributed by Louise Robert, Designed by Lucy Pankurst

0854   Baby Hat, Contributed by Angela Tong, Designed by Gro

0859 | Snuggle Time Baby, Designed & Contributed by Terry Liann Morris

0858 | Cubba, Designed & Contributed by Woolly Wormhead

0860 | Simple Baby Hat, Contributed by Angela Tong, Designed by Susan B. Anderson

0861   Charlotte's Web, Contributed by Tot Toppers,
Designed by Kathryn L. Oates

0862   Bunny Hat,
Contributed by Alexandra Johnson

0863   Skull Hat, Contributed by Ruth Moline,
Designed by Adrian Bizilia

0865 | Gulf Shores Hat, Contributed by
Mandy Furney, Designed by Melissa Rotert

0866 | Striped Ball Cap, Contributed by Tot Toppers,
Designed by Kathryn L. Oates

Photo by KSC Photography

0864 | Black Baby Witch's Hat, Contributed by
Mandy Furney, Designed by Cheryl Oxsalida

0867 | Striped Ball Hat, Contributed by the SWTC Collection, Designed by Jonelle Raffino

0869 | Cupcake Preemie Hat, Contributed by Constance M. Cole, Designed by Labpugglechi

0868 | Striped Stocking, Designed & Contributed by Michelle Kennedy

0870 | Baby Hat, Designed & Contributed by Jane Nowakowski

0871 | Giggles Hat, Contributed by Shelley D. Jones, Designed by Terry Liann Morris

0872 | Hat the First, Contributed by A.M.

0873 | Norwegian Sweet Baby Hat, Contributed by Mandy Furney, Designed by Gro

0875 | Sam the Man, Designed & Contributed by Debby Ware

0874 | Colorwork Watch Cap, Designed & Contributed by Annie Modesitt

0876 | Slip Stitch Pixie Hat, Designed & Contributed by Lexi Boeger

0877 | Gingerbread House Hat, Designed & Contributed by Terry Liann Morris

0879 | Tie Hat, Contributed by ChezPlum, Designed by Sylvie Damey

0878 | Carousel Hat, Designed & Contributed by Lizette Hopkins

0880 | Garter Stripe, Contributed by Louise Robert

0882 | Purple Fair Isle, Contributed by
Michelle Tibbs & Elizabeth Cadieux

0883 | Ultimate Fan Hat, Contributed by Tot Toppers,
Designed by Kathryn L. Oates

0881 | Infant's Colorwork Topper, Designed & Contributed
by Anne E. P. Boyer, Designed by Anne Boyer

0884 | Cream Pink Multi, Contributed by Michelle Tibbs & Elizabeth Cadieux

0886 | Wide Purple Stripe, Contributed by Michelle Tibbs & Elizabeth Cadieux

0885 | Felted Purple Stripe, Contributed by Michelle Tibbs & Elizabeth Cadieux

0887 | Felted Infant's Pillbox, Designed & Contributed by Anne E. P. Boyer

0890 | Civil War Cap,
Contributed by Lobug Designs

0889 | Elephant Beret, Designed &
Contributed by Michelle Kennedy

0888 | Basketweave Hat, Designed &
Contributed by Joanne Seiff

0894 | Cabled Teddy Bear Hat, Contributed by
Carolyn Vance, Designed by Julie Hentz

0892 | Kiki Hat, Contributed by ChezPlum,
Designed by Sylvie Damey

0891 | Fuzzy Green Beret, Contributed by
Michelle Kennedy, Designed by Kenzie Graham

0893 | Tasseled Fez, Contributed by Mandy Powers,
Designed by Charlene Schurch

0897   **Checkered Square Topper, Contributed by Tot Toppers, Designed by Kathryn L. Oates**
Photo by KSC Photography

0895   **Orange Baseball Stitching, Contributed by Michelle Tibbs & Elizabeth Cadieux**

0896   **Starry Stripes, Designed & Contributed by Dana Lorz**

0900 | Thin Blue Bands, Contributed by Michelle Tibbs & Elizabeth Cadieux

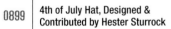

0899 | 4th of July Hat, Designed & Contributed by Hester Sturrock

0898 | Allover Fair Isle, Contributed by Michelle Tibbs & Elizabeth Cadieux

0901 | Stripes & Dots, Contributed by Tot Toppers, Designed by Kathryn L. Oates

Photo by KSC Photography

0902 | Baby's Colorwork, Designed & Contributed by Anne E. P. Boyer

0904 | Apple Hat, Contributed by Kate JK Smith

0903 | Spidey Tamberet, Designed & Contributed by Helen Jacobs-Grant

Photo by Lionel Jacobs

0905 | Adjustable Baby Hat, Designed & Contributed by Sherry Heit

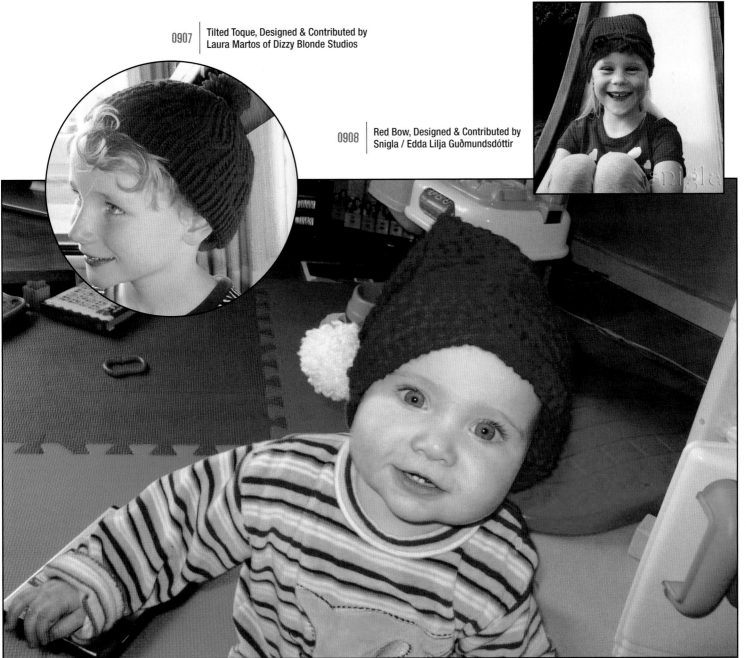

0907 | Tilted Toque, Designed & Contributed by
Laura Martos of Dizzy Blonde Studios

0908 | Red Bow, Designed & Contributed by
Snigla / Edda Lilja Guðmundsdóttir

0906 | Baby's Hat, Designed &
Contributed by Isabelle Boutin

0910 | Grape Fizz, Designed &
Contributed by Bonnie Franz

0912 | 1920s' Child Hat, Designed
& Contributed by Michelle Kennedy

0909 | Baby Tri-Peak, Designed &
Contributed by Woolly Wormhead

0911 | 1920s' Child Hat, Designed
& Contributed by Michelle Kennedy

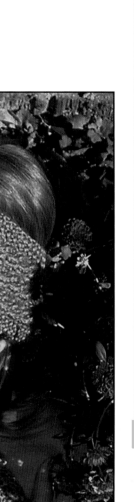

0914 | Chevron Lace Baby Hat, Contributed by
Lies Spaink, Designed by Jinjifore

0913 | Cable & Seed Baby Hat, Contributed
by Angela Tong, Designed by Sundara Murphy

0915 | Simply Soft Ear and Hand Warmers, Designed &
Contributed by Kelly Klem of Klymyshyn Design

0917 | Double Layer Mesh, Designed & Contributed by Snigla / Edda Lilja Guðmundsdóttir

0916 | Autumn Bands, Contributed by Michelle Tibbs & Elizabeth Cadieux

0918 | Crown, Contributed by Jennifer Johnson, Designed by Jennifer Peters

0921 | Elf, Designed &
Contributed by Edie Eckman

0920 | Lattice Kerchief, Contributed by Rebecca Mercier,
Designed by Magistra Lanam Amat

0919 | Wide Brown Band, Contributed by
Michelle Tibbs & Elizabeth Cadieux

0922 | Baby Hat, Designed &
Contributed by Lorna Pearman

0923 Carousel Beret, Designed & Contributed by Connie Haney

0925 Elfin Lace Hat, Contributed by Alexandra Johnson

0926 Baby Hat, Contributed by Rebecca Mercier, Designed by Julie Hentz

0924 Yellow Grey Triangles, Contributed by Michelle Tibbs & Elizabeth Cadieux

0927 | Inca Cap, Designed & Contributed by Michelle Kennedy

0928 | Knight Hood, Designed & Contributed by Jennifer Small

0929 | Tubey, Designed & Contributed by Woolly Wormhead

0930 | Blue & Yellow with Bee, Contributed by Michelle Tibbs & Elizabeth Cadieux

0932 | Baby's First Argyles, Designed & Contributed by Bonnie Franz

0931 | Child's Intarsia Pillbox, Designed & Contributed by Anne E. P. Boyer

0933 | Eyelets & Bobbles Hat, Designed & Contributed by Terry Liann Morris

0934 | Curlique Crochet Baby Hat, Designed &
Contributed by Essie Woods Bruell

0935 | Buttercup Lace Cap, Contributed by
Tot Toppers, Designed by Kathryn L. Oates

0936 | Ganomy Hat for Child, Contributed by
Mandy Powers, Designed by Elizabeth Zimmerman

0937 | Cupcake, Designed & Contributed by Woolly Wormhead

0938 | Watermelon Cap, Designed & Contributed by Michele Lee Bernstein, PDXKnitterati

0939 | Kaleidoscope Hat, Designed & Contributed by Michelle Kennedy

0941 | Sweet Lace, Designed & Contributed by Bonnie Franz

0942 | Rosayah hat, Contributed by ChezPlum, Designed by Sylvie Damey

0940 | Friday's Hat, Contributed by Carolyn Vance, Designed by Jacqueline Fee

0943 | Candy Cap, Designed & Contributed by Essie Woods Bruell

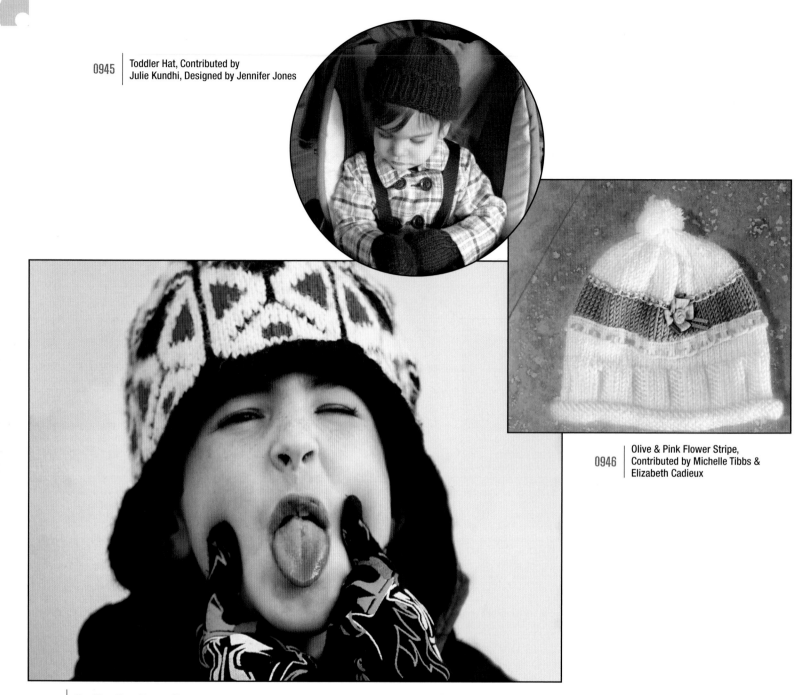

0945 | Toddler Hat, Contributed by
Julie Kundhi, Designed by Jennifer Jones

0946 | Olive & Pink Flower Stripe,
Contributed by Michelle Tibbs &
Elizabeth Cadieux

0944 | Star Wars Clone Trooper Hat,
Designed & Contributed by Erin Taylor Bell

0950 | Basic Ribbed Hat, Designed & Contributed by Hester Sturrock

0948 | Kaylee Hat, Designed & Contributed by Mandy Furney

0947 | Socks and Hats, Designed & Contributed by Julie Witt

0949 | Safari Sun Hat, Contributed by Tot Toppers, Designed by Kathryn L. Oates

Photo by KSC Photography

0952 | Pearl's 1st Birthday Hat, Designed & Contributed by Lee Meredith

0954 | Child's Hat, Contributed by Kimberly Nico, Designed by Daniel Yuhas

Photo by Renae Hwang

0951 | Madison Hat, Designed & Contributed by Tina Whitmore for Knitwhits

0953 | Striped Hood, Designed & Contributed by Michelle Kennedy

0955 | Novelty Disco Beret, Contributed by ChezPlum, Designed by Sylvie Damey

0957 | Welt Hat, Designed & Contributed by Carolyn Vance

0956 | Old-Fashioned Bonnet, Contributed by Alexandra Johnson, Designed by Larissa Brown

0958 | Kid's Hat, Contributed by Dana K. Smith, Designed by Gina Doherty

0960 | Grey / Black Pointer, Designed & Contributed by Snigla / Edda Lilja Guðmundsdóttir

0961 | Zebra Hat, Contributed by the SWTC Collection, Designed by Pinka Peck

0959 | Ostrich Headscarf, Designed & Contributed by Catherine Bursell

0963 | Raccoon Cap, Designed &
Contributed by Annie Modesitt

0964 | Alpine Hats, Designed &
Contributed by Terry Liann Morris

0962 | Ollie Hat, Designed & Contributed
by Tina Whitmore for Knitwhits

0965 | Growing Baby Hat, Designed &
Contributed by Alexandra Johnson

0966 | Pink with Multi Striping, Contributed by Michelle Tibbs & Elizabeth Cadieux

0969 | Soft and Simple, Designed & Contributed by Edie Eckman

0967 | Girl's Hat & Mittens, Designed & Contributed by AnneLena K. Mattison

0968 | Miss Dashwood, Contributed by Sarah Fay, Designed by Heather Ramsay

0971 | The Amanda Hat, Designed
& Contributed by Gina House

0972 | Baby Loops, Contributed by Patricia Would,
Cottonon, Designed by Woolly Wormhead

0970 | Cozy Baby Hat, Designed &
Contributed by Margaret Hubert

Knit Over Flowers 2,
Contributed by A.M.

0973 | Bobbled Band, Contributed by
Michelle Tibbs & Elizabeth Cadieux

0974 | Trio of Baby Caps, Contributed by Michelle Tibbs
& Elizabeth Cadieux

0978 | Baby Hat, Contributed by
Marie Stanley, That 80's Hat

0977 | Purple Flower Stripe, Contributed by
Michelle Tibbs & Elizabeth Cadieux

0976 | Orange Daisy Stripe, Contributed by
Michelle Tibbs & Elizabeth Cadieux

0979 | Buttery Beanie, Designed &
Contributed by Debby Ware

0982 | Blue Daisy, Contributed by
Michelle Tibbs & Elizabeth Cadieux

0980 | Baby's Hat, Contributed by Mandy Furney,
Designed by Gayle Beroit

0981 | 4 Sports Caps, Contributed by
Michelle Tibbs & Elizabeth Cadieux

0983 | Tiffany Cap, Contributed by
Michelle Tibbs & Elizabeth Cadieux

0985 | Corny Surprise Hat, Contributed by
Janice M. Hamby, TwinSet Designs,
Designed by Gina House

0984 | Grey Elephant, Designed &
Contributed by Heather Broadhurst

0986 | Ruffled Brim Ribbon Hat,
Contributed by Lies Spaink

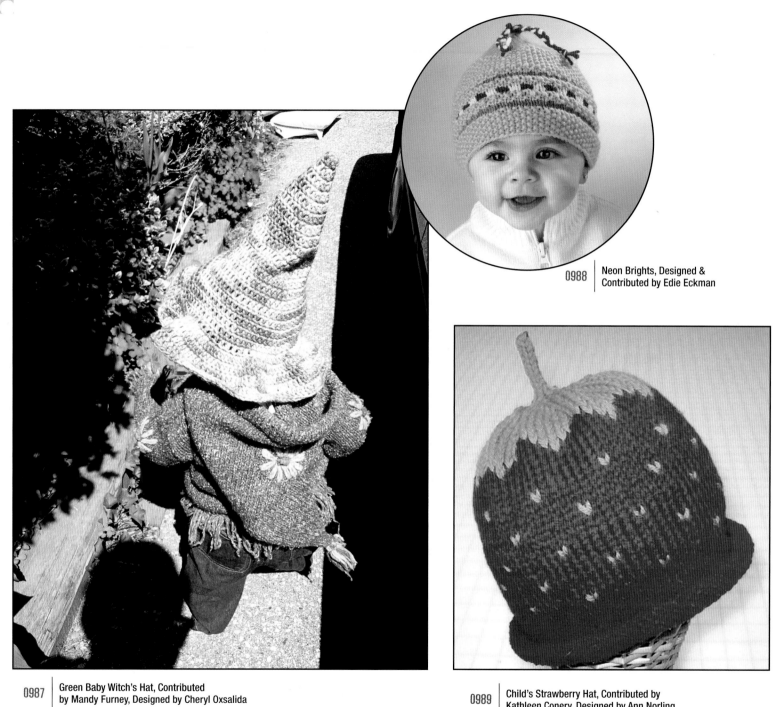

0988 | Neon Brights, Designed & Contributed by Edie Eckman

0987 | Green Baby Witch's Hat, Contributed by Mandy Furney, Designed by Cheryl Oxsalida

0989 | Child's Strawberry Hat, Contributed by Kathleen Conery, Designed by Ann Norling

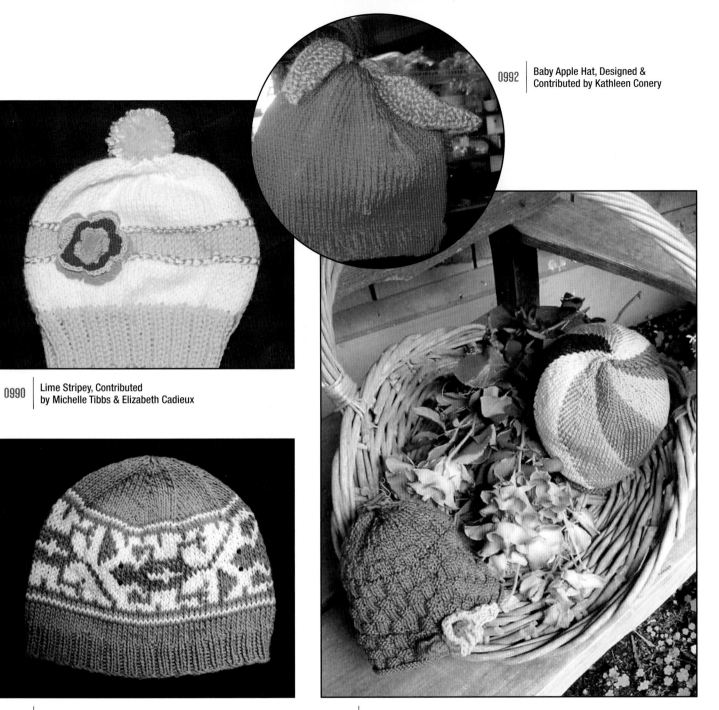

0992 | Baby Apple Hat, Designed & Contributed by Kathleen Conery

0990 | Lime Stripey, Contributed by Michelle Tibbs & Elizabeth Cadieux

0991 | Baby Hat, Designed & Contributed by Lorna Pearman

0993 | HoneyRose & Ollie, Designed & Contributed by Tina Whitmore for Knitwhits

0995 | Child's Hat,
Contributed by Irene Armock

0996 | Cesia's Hat, Designed &
Contributed by Anne Kuo Lukito

0994 | Sweet Jester, Contributed by Tot Toppers,
Designed by Kathryn L. Oates
Photo by KSC Photography

0997 | Baby Pixie Hat,
Contributed by Mandy Furney

0998 | Hobbit Hat, Designed & Contributed by Kelly Klem of Klymyshyn Design

0999 | Pom-Pom Baby Hat, Designed & Contributed by Terry Liann Morris

1000 | Samantha Hat, Designed & Contributed by Katie Harmon, PinkPolish Design

Information for All Patterns

Stitch Definitions

Used in more than one pattern. Stitches used for only one pattern will be explained in that pattern only.

K2tog-L: knit 2 sts together so they slant to the left when viewed from RS of work (aka SSK, k2togTBL or s1, k1, psso)

K2tog-R: Knit 2 sts together so they slant to the right when viewed from RS of work (aka k2tog)

kfb - Knit into the Front and Back: Knit into the front and back of one stitch, then kick that stitch off the needle. (Increase of 1 st.)

M1 - Make One Stitch: Pick up the horizontal loop between next 2 sts, place it onto LH needle, then knit into the back of it

Sl 1 yRS: Move yarn to RS of work. Insert RH needle purlwise into st and slip off of LH needle.

Sl 1 yWS: Move yarn to WS of work. Insert RH needle purlwise into st and slip off of LH needle.

St st: Knit on right side, purl on wrong side

VDD - Vertical Double Decrease: Sl 2 sts as if to work k2 tog R, k1, pass slipped sts over (decrease of 2 sts)

YO - Yarn-Over: Wrap yarn around hook or needle

Special Techniques

Used in more than one pattern. Techniques used for only one pattern will be explained in that pattern only.

I-Cord: Using a circular or double pointed needle, cast on desired number of sts. Knit these sts, do NOT turn.

Slide the sts to the opposite end of the needle and knit the sts again. The yarn will be coming from the last st on the needle; this is correct. Repeat.

Tug on cord to block out the gap. When cord is desired length, cut yarn and pull through sts to tie off.

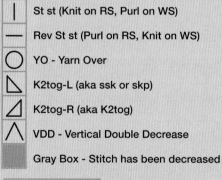

	St st (Knit on RS, Purl on WS)
	Rev St st (Purl on RS, Knit on WS)
	YO - Yarn Over
	K2tog-L (aka ssk or skp)
	K2tog-R (aka K2tog)
	VDD - Vertical Double Decrease
	Gray Box - Stitch has been decreased

 C4L - Cable 4 Left (aka Cable 4 Front)

section 3

winning Patterns

0001

Flowers
Harpa Jónsdóttir

Our winning hat is a brilliant combination of knitting, felting, and embroidery.

Notes: *The hat is felted. It is stretched and formed to fit when wet, so it fits a variety of heads. The embroidery is not nearly as hard as it might look. But it does—as most good things—take some time.*

About the yarn: *Istex Plötulopi is an unspun Icelandic new wool roving that can be worked one, two, or more plies at a time, depending on how bulky a yarn you want.*

Gently wind the required number of strands together into a ball by taking the end from the center and the end from the outside of the plate, or plates. Plötulopi is very fragile to knit. A good substitute would be a very soft single-ply yarn like Malabrigo Merino or Lamb's Pride Worsted, but the effect may be dramatically different than the original hat.

For this project it is best to keep the tension very loose. If the yarn breaks, simply overlap the ends a bit and continue as if nothing had happened.

Sizes: Small (Medium, Large)
Finished Meas: To fit head size 20 (22, 23)"/52 (56, 58.5)cm
Sample Size: Small
Skill Level: K 2 Easy

Fiber: Istex Plötulopi (328yds/300m, 3.85oz/110gr) per skein
    Yarn A - Dk Brown Heather 1032, 1 ball
    Yarn B - Brown Heather 0009, 1 ball
    Yarn C - White 0001, 2 balls
    (www.istex.is)

Needles: Size US 10/6mm, 16"/40.5cm long circular needle and double-pointed needles (dpns) or size needed to achieve gauge

Gauge: Exact gauge is not important because the hat is felted. But it should be knit loosely, so if you know yourself to be a tight knitter, you should consider choosing one size bigger knitting needles.

Notions: Tapestry needle, sharp embroidery needle, stitch marker, three safety pins

DMC Strand Embroidery Floss:
One skein of each in the following colors (or your choice):

    350 MD Coral
    351 Coral
    352 LT Coral
    353 Peach
    369 V LT Pistachio Green
    420 DK Hazelnut Brown
    435 V LT Brown
    436 Tan
    437 LT Tan
    564 V LT Jade
    581 Moss Green
    721 MD Orange Spice
    722 LT Orange Spice
    725 MD LT Topaz
    727 V LT Topaz
    744 Pale Yellow
    743 MD Yellow
    783 MD Topaz
    921 Copper
    972 Deep Canary
    3078 V LT Golden Yellow
    3779 Ultra V LT Terra-Cotta
    3805 Cyclamen Pink

Preparation: Creating the Balls
Note: *If you're using a plied yarn that is already in balls, skip this step. If you are using the suggested yarn or knitting from roving, wind the balls in the following manner:*

Wind up a small single-ply ball of the darker brown yarn; it should be roughly the size of an American baseball. Break the yarn; set the ball aside.

Taking the strand from both the inside and the outside of the plate of roving, wind a 2-ply ball of the dark brown. This ball should be the size of a softball, a bit bigger than the first.

Wind the remaining dark brown wool into a 2-ply ball. You should now have three dark brown balls: one single ply and two larger balls, both 2-ply.

Wind the white and light brown yarn into 2-ply balls.

You can also knit directly from the wheels. If you are knitting from a single wheel, it is easiest to take the inner and outer strand (shown in the picture of the pink wheel).

Brim
With the larger 2-ply dark brown ball and circular needle, CO 72 (84, 96) sts and join, being careful not to twist the work. Place a stitch marker to note the start of round.

Join the smaller 2-ply ball and knit 3 rounds with all 4 strands (ply) of wool. Break the yarn from the smaller ball and add the single-ply ball. Knit 3 rounds with 3 strands of wool. Break the yarn from the single-ply yarn and continue knitting 2 rounds with 2 strands of dark brown wool, then break the wool.

From this point on the hat is knit with 2-ply wool.

Knit 4 rounds with 2 ply of lighter brown; break light brown.

Knit 8 (8¾, 9½)"/20 (22, 24)cm with white.

Crown Decrease
Note: *When the circumference becomes too small for the circular needle, switch to dpns.*

Next round (1st dec round): *K10, k2tog; rep from * around—66 (77, 88) sts.

Knit 3 (4, 4) rounds.

Next round (2nd dec round): *K9, k2tog; rep from * around—60 (70, 80) sts.

Knit 3 (4, 4) rounds.

Next round (3rd dec round): *K8, k2tog; rep from * around—54 (63, 72) sts.

Knit 3 rounds (all sizes).

Next round (4th dec round): *K7, k2tog; rep from * around—48 (56, 64) sts.

Knit 2 (3, 3) rounds.

Next round (5th dec round): *K6, k2tog; rep from * around—42 (49, 56) sts.

Knit 2 (3, 3) rounds.

Next round (6th dec round): *K5, k2tog; rep from * around—36 (42, 48) sts.

Knit 1 (2, 2) rounds.

Next round (7th dec round): *K4, k2tog; rep from * around—30 (35, 40) sts.

Knit 1 round (all sizes).

Next round (8th dec round): *K3, k2tog; rep from * around—24 (28, 32) sts.

Knit 1 round (all sizes).

Next round (9th dec round): *K2, k2tog; rep from * around—18 (21, 24) sts.

Next round (10th dec round): *K1, k2tog; rep from * around—12 (14, 16) sts.

Next round (11th dec round): *K2tog; rep from * around—6 (7, 8) sts.

Knit 8 rounds. Thread the yarn through the remaining sts and pull carefully. Weave the ends in on the wrong side.

Tip

Now the hat is really big, floppy, and probably uneven, too. Don't worry; everything is as it should be.

Felting

There are two schools of thought on felting: hand felting and machine felting. Machine felting is much faster, but requires some care because each machine felts differently. So my advice

is use a short cycle, start with low heat 104°F (40°C), and increase if that is not enough. It is a good idea to use a washing bag or something similar to protect your machine and two old towels or so to increase agitation. Spin very carefully to avoid creases. When done you should have a dense, even fabric and the hat should be somewhat smaller than you want it to be in the end. It will probably look like a mess at this stage but never worry—this is the time to mold it to the shape you want. Form the wet hat on your own head, or on the person who is to wear it, if at all possible. Heads vary widely in size! Curl up the edge and pull the top up straight. Don't be afraid to use a little force; the felted fabric can stand a lot of tugging and pulling. Let it dry standing.

To hand felt you need a basin or a sink filled with hot water. Add a few drops of dishwashing liquid and use your hands to swish the wool around in the water and rub it together. You need quite a lot of agitation, so rubber gloves are a good idea. They can also add an extra bit of roughness if you use gloves with textured palms. Felting by hand can take a long time, so patience is the key. When you are done, rinse the hat well, squeeze out most of the water, form as described above, and let it dry standing.

Embroidery

The embroidery drawings are in black and white, and the colors of the lines and flowers are written along each line. The colors stated in the materials list are the ones used in the sample, but feel free to alter or minimize this list if you like.

In fact, I would like to encourage you to consider the color of your eyes (or the intended wearer's eyes) for a moment. What color really makes them shine? And what colors complement that color? Your unique beautiful palette will soon reveal itself.

There are only three types of stitches in this hat:

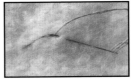

Stem stitch

Stem Stitch (see image)

This stitch has many names, among them crewel stitch or stalk stitch. It is worked from the left to the right taking small regular stitches with a forward and backward motion. Bring the thread up from the back of the fabric on the line you want to stitch. Make a stitch forward and bring the needle up, a little to the back of the first stitch. Pull the thread through the fabric. Make the second stitch forward, bringing the needle out a little to the back of the second stitch. Repeat, keeping the thread always on the right of the needle.

French Knot (see image)

Bring the needle out through the fabric and hold the thread taut. With your right hand twist the needle around the thread three times (or two times—or four—whatever you like). Still holding the thread firmly, take the needle back into the fabric, a very short space away from where the floss emerges from the fabric, and insert the needle. Pull carefully to form the knot. In this project it adds visual interest to use different size (that is, number of twists) knots.

Daisy Stitch (see image)

Also called the detached chain stitch, this is often used to make leaves, flowers, and similar things. To work this stitch, first bring the needle up through the fabric and hold the thread with the left thumb. Then insert the needle back into

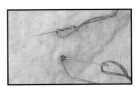

French knot

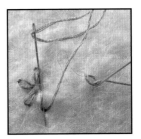

Daisy stitch

where it first came out. Take the needle through the fabric, taking the point of the needle out a short space away. With the thread wrapped under the needle point, pull the needle through the fabric. Fasten the loop made with a small stitch.

The total floss strands are divided in half throughout—that is, you work with three strands at a time. Cut a comfortable length of floss each time, 47"/120cm or so, even if you are only going to stitch a little flower or a short line. You use up the rest by making leaves and seeds (French knots) in the neighborhood.

Don't stitch all the way through the fabric. All the ends should be hidden securely and invisibly inside the felted wool and you should only stitch about halfway through. Nothing should be visible on the inside. That way the hat keeps its warmth and softness.

Divide the brim of the hat into three sections and put a safety pin in each "corner." Now you have three reference points, because the embroidery drawing is in three parts.

One way to tackle the embroidery is to start with the lines. Use the drawing as a guide: there is no need to be exact, let the lines flow, and make them your own. The pattern is not the law—you are the boss. Embroider all the way down, even if you think the brim will cover it. Gaps there will show when the hat is worn.

When you are done with a length of line and there is time to switch colors, finish off the length of the floss by making seeds and leaves randomly around the line and the neighboring lines. Take care not to put too many leaves or seeds in the same color together; spread them out to get more visual interest. All the colors are used for leaves and seeds.

Place the bigger flowers first, then the smaller ones. Make leaves and seeds "on the way" as you did with the lines. When you are done, look at your hat. Does it need more leaves? Are there any gaps? Fill in where needed with leaves and seeds or more lines and flowers.

Enjoy your new hat!

End of May Hat
Mandy Powers

Colorwork is one of the joys of knitting, and this hat demonstrates several wonderful techniques (knitted facing, stranded colorwork, and beautiful top decreasing).

Notes: *Markers placed between pattern repeats are optional, but they are helpful in keeping track of the large repeat. A distinct beginning of round marker is helpful to remind you when to switch to the next round.*

For a shorter hat, begin on row 17 of the chart. Use size US 3 (3.25mm) needles to create a smaller hat to fit a size 18½"/47cm head. Larger needles and a heavier yarn can be used with this chart to create a larger hat.

Hat Section 1

Hat Section 2

Hat Section 3

Flowers Embroidery Charts

Size: One Size
Finished Meas: To fit head size 22"/56cm
Skill Level: K 3 Intermediate

Fiber: Berroco, Ultra Alpaca (215yds/196m, 3.5oz/100gr) per skein
    Yarn A - Cordoba Grape 6212, 1 ball
    Yarn B - Dijon 6253, 1 ball
    Yarn C - Ultra Alpaca Light, Lavender Mix 4283, 1 ball
    (144yds /131m, 1.75oz /50gr)
    (www.berroco.com)

Needles: Size US 5/3.75mm, 16"/40.5cm long circular and double-pointed needles (dpns) or size needed to achieve gauge

Gauge: 24 sts and 27 rows = 4"/10cm in Stranded Work using size US 5/3.75mm circular or double-pointed needles

Notions: Stitch markers (4), blunt and sharp darning needles

Facing

With C and circular needle, CO 120 sts using the long tail method. Place marker (PM). Join into the round without twisting. Work around in St st (knit every round) until piece measures 2"/5cm. Break yarn. Join in A and knit one round. Purl one round and at the same time, PM every 30 sts to mark patt rep, using contrasting marker to note start of round.

Sideband

Join B and starting with row 1 of chart, work chart four times around all sts. Work rows 1–62 of the Colorwork Chart, changing to dpns when too few sts rem to use the circular needle. At the end of chart 16 sts rem.

Finishing

Cut both yarns. Use the blunt darning needle to draw A through the live sts, securing them. Weave in all ends. Use the sharp darning needle and A to sew facing to underside of hat, being careful not to let the sewing thread show through to the right side. Wet block. Use a head form or lay flat to dry.

Main Color
Contrast Color
No Stitch
K2tog-L
K2tog-R

End of May Hat Colorwork Chart

0003

Is It Spring Yet?

Constance M. Cole

Inspired by the Grun ist die Hoffnung sock pattern by Stephanie Van der Linden, the designer adapted the pattern (with permission) to create a hat.

Notes: This hat is knit from the top down, beginning on double-pointed needles (dpns) and switching to circular, if you wish. The chart represents one-fifth of the entire pattern; it is repeated five times around the circumference of the hat.

Size: One Size
Finished Meas: To fit head size 21"/53.25cm
Skill Level: K 3 Intermediate

Fiber: King Cole Bounty (800yds/730m, 8.75oz/250gr) per skein
    Color - Fondant, 128, 1 ball

Needles: Size US 6/4mm, 16"/40.5cm long circular and double-pointed needles (dpns) or size needed to achieve gauge

Gauge: 24 sts and 32 rows = 4"/10cm in St st using needle size US 6/4mm, 16"/40.5cm long circular needle

Notions: Darning needle, set of dpns or second circular needle for tip of hat

Crown

With dpns, CO 5 sts.
    Inc into each st by knitting into the front and back of each st; place marker to mark beg of round and join—10 sts, 5 sections of 2 sts each.
    Beg with round 1 of chart, work Lace Chart through round 49—110 sts.

Note: *When two YOs are side by side, work these by knitting into the front and back of each YO in the following round. At the end of the chart, work 1 round even in St st with no inc or dec.*

Note: *Only odd-numbered rounds are shown on chart; on even-numbered rounds, work sts as they present themselves with no incs or decs.*

Band

Work around in k1, p1 ribbing.

For a tighter band, especially if using a "loose" yarn like bamboo, you may wish to switch to smaller needles, dec 2 sts evenly around work (108 sts rem) and work in a k2, p2 ribbing for a snugger fit.

Work 12 rounds of ribbing, or work to desired length. BO loosely in rib pattern.

Finishing

Weave in any yarn ends. Block as desired.

0004

Lavender Lattice

Mary Keenan

To achieve the effect of an oversized petit-four, the designer has used a variation of Threaded Stitch and Quilted Lattice, as shared by Barbara G. Walker in *A Treasury of Knitting Patterns*.

Notes: *To minimize any pattern jogging on either side of the start-of-row marker, use duplicate stitch embroidery to finish that area of the hat.*

Sizes: Women's Small (Medium, Large)
Finished Meas: To fit head size 21 (22, 23)"/53.8 (56.4, 59)cm
Hat Depth: 7 (7½, 8)"/17.9 (19.2, 20.5)cm
Sample Size: Medium, 22"/56cm
Skill Level: K 4 Advanced

Fiber: Elsebeth Lavold, Silky Wool (190yds/173m, 1.75oz /50gr) per skein
    Yarn A - Lava, 1 ball
    Yarn B - Lime Juice, 1 ball

Needles: Sizes US 3/3.25mm and US 4/3.5mm, 16"/40.5cm long circular or double-pointed needles (dpns) or size needed to achieve gauge

Notions: Darning needle, stitch marker

Gauge: 21 sts and 28 rows = 4"/10cm in Royal Quilting Stitch using size US 3/3.25mm circular or double-pointed needle

Special Stitches:
sl wyRS = slip with yarn on right side
sl wyWS = slip with yarn on wrong side

SPECIAL TECHNIQUES

Duplicate Stitch Embroidery: A method of embroidery that appears to be knit into the fabric. Worked by duplicating a previously knit stitch in a new color.

Thread a darning needle with the new color of yarn.

Draw needle from the back to the front through the center of the stitch BELOW the stitch you want to duplicate (Stitch X). Slip the needle under both legs of Stitch X. Pull the needle to the back through the center of the stitch below Stitch X, exactly where you started the stitch. Repeat from * to * for each stitch.

KStF - Knit Second through First: Slip RH needle through first stitch on LH needle as if to purl, then knit the second stitch on LH needle. Leaving it on the needle, knit the first stitch through its back loop.

PUL - Pick Up Loop: Using the tip of the RH needle, pick up the loop left in front during a previous row and slip it behind the next stitch on the LH needle so that it rests between the first two stitches on LH needle.

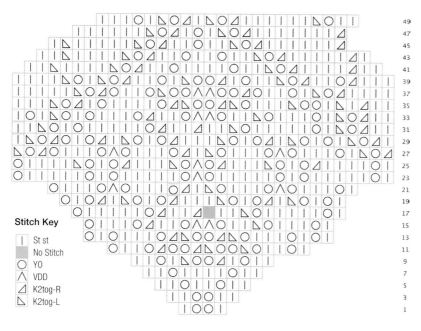

Stitch Key

	St st
	No Stitch
O	YO
/\	VDD
◿	K2tog-R
◺	K2tog-L

Is It Spring Yet? Lace Chart

Band

Using size 3 needles and A, CO 102 (108, 114) sts. Divide onto dpns with a multiple of 3 sts on each needle (st counts on each needle will not be equal). Place marker, making sure you leave a multiple of 3 sts to the left of it.

Round 1: With size 4 needle on the right, *k2, p1; rep from * to end.

Round 2: With size 3 needle on the right, *k 2nd st through, k 1st st, p1; rep from * to end. (Be sure to work both sts before transferring them to the right needle, because it is very easy to forget to knit the 1st st and very difficult to pick it up again on subsequent rows.)

Rep these 2 rows until the ribbing measures 1¼ (1½, 1½)"/3 (4, 4)cm, ending with a row 1. Continue with size 3 needles only.

Royal Quilting Crown

Round 1: With A, [k1, sl 2 wyWS] twice, *k1, sl 5 wyRS; rep from * to last 6 sts, (k1, sl 2 wyWS) twice.

Rounds 2–4: With B, k.

Round 5: With A, (k1, sl 2 wyWS) twice, *k1, sl 2 wyWS, PUL, k1, sl 2 wyWS; rep from * to last 6 sts, (k1, sl 2 wyWS) twice.

Round 6: With A, k1, sl 2 wyWS, *k1, sl 5 wyRS; rep from * to last 3 sts, k1, sl 2 wyWS.

Rounds 7–9: With B, k.

Round 10: With A, k1, sl 2 wyWS, *k1, sl 2 wyWS, PUL, k1, sl 2 wyWS; rep from * to last 3 sts, k1, sl 2 wyWS.

Rep these 10 rounds twice more.

Hat Body Decreases

Round 1: With A, (k1, sl 2 wyWS) twice, *k1, sl 5 wyRS; rep from * to last 6 sts, (k1, sl 2 wyRS) twice.

Rounds 2–3: With B, k.

Round 4: With B, *k32 (10, 17), K2tog-R; rep from * to end—99 (99, 108) sts.

Round 5 (Small Only): With A, (k1, sl 2 wyWS) twice, (k1, sl 2 wyWS, PUL, K1, sl 2 wyWS) 4 times, k1, sl 1 wyWS, PUL, k1, sl 2 wyWS, (k1, sl 2 wyWS, PUL, k1, sl 2 wyWS) 5 times, k1, sl 1 wyWS, PUL, k1, sl 2 wyWS, (k1, sl 2 wyWS, PUL, k1, sl 2 wyWS, PUL, k1, sl 2 wyWS) 4 times, k1, sl 2 wyWS, PUL, k1, sl 1 wyWS.

Round 5 (Medium Only): With A, (k1, sl 2 wyWS) twice, *k1, sl 2 wyWS, PUL, k1, sl 1 wyWS, k1, sl 2 wyWS, PUL, k1, sl 2 wyWS; rep from * to last 3 sts, end k1, sl 2 wyWS.

Round 5 (Large Only): With A, (k1, sl 2 wyWS) twice, k1, sl 2 wyWS, PUL, k1, sl 2 wyWS, k1, sl 2 wyWS, PUL, k1, sl 1 wyWS, (k1, sl 2 wyWS, PUL, k1, sl 2 wyWS) 3 times, [k1, sl 1 wyWS, PUL, k1, sl 2 wyWS, (k1, sl 2 wyWS, PUL, k1, sl 2 wyWS) twice] four times, end k1, sl 2 wyWS, PUL, k1, sl 1 wyWS.

Crown Decreases

Round 1: With A, *k9 (9, 10), K2tog-R; rep from * to end—90 (90, 99) sts.

Rounds 2, 4, 6, 8: With A, k to end.

Round 3: With A, *k8 (8, 9), K2tog-R; rep from * to end—81 (81, 90) sts.

Round 5: With A, *k7 (7, 8), K2tog-R; rep from * to end—72 (72, 81) sts.

Round 7: With A, *k6 (6, 7), K2tog-R; rep from * to end—63 (63, 72) sts.

Round 9: With A, *k5 (5, 6), K2tog-R; rep from * to end—54 (54, 63) sts.

Round 10: *With B, k0 (0, 0), with A, k4 (6, 7); rep from * to end.

Round 11: *With B, k0 (0, 0), with A, k2 (4, 5), K2tog-R; rep from * to end—45 (45, 54) sts.

Round 12: *With B, k1 (1, 0), with A, k3 (4, 6); rep from * to end.

Round 13: *With B, k1 (1, 0), with A, k1 (2, 4), K2tog-R; rep from * to end—36 (36, 45) sts.

Round 14: *With B, k1, with A, k3 (3, 4); rep from * to end.

Round 15: *With B, k1, with A, k1 (1, 2), K2tog-R; rep from * to end—27 (27, 36) sts.

Round 16: *With B, k1, with A, k1 (1, 2); rep from * to end.

Round 17: *With B, k1, with A, k0 (0, 1), K2tog-R; rep from * to end—18 (18, 27) sts.
Note: Sizes S and M end.

Round 18 (Large Only): *With B, k1, with A, k2; rep from * to end.

Round 19 (Large Only): *With B, k1, with A, K2tog-R; rep from * to end—18 sts.
Note: Size L ends.

Finishing

Break yarns A and B, leaving an 8"/20.5cm tail. With darning needle, thread A through rem 18 sts. Turn hat inside out to pull sts tight. Weave both tails into WS of hat.

Using a strand of A and darning needle, use duplicate stitch embroidery to fill in any sts or lattice marks missing from the patt near the beg or end of each round. Weave in rem ends and block.

0005

Altay Hat
Kureyon
ChezPlum

Granny squares are a favorite of Sylvie Damey; this hat is worked around a "triangle granny square," using different stitches to shape the hat. The hat is made using a rather unusual construction—there are no decreases, and shaping is achieved through the consecutive use of tall and short stitches. This works up very quickly and is easily adjustable to suit anybody's head size.

Sizes: Small (Medium, Large)
Finished Meas: To fit head size 20 (22, 23")/50 (55, 58)cm
Sample Size: Small
Skill Level: C 2 Easy

Yarn A

Small: Noro, Kureyon Sock (462yds/421m, 3.5oz/100gr), 1 ball in Moss
Medium: Noro Kureyon (110yds/100m, 1.75oz/50gr), 1 ball in Moss
Large: Noro Silk Garden (122yds/411m, 1.75oz/50gr), 1 ball in Purple Mix

Yarn B

Small amount (approx 40–80 yds/37–73m) of a contrasting yarn the same weight as Yarn A.

Needles: Size US H-8/5mm crochet hook for Small; size US J-9/6mm crochet hook for Medium; size US K-10½/6.5mm crochet hook for Large or size needed to achieve gauge

Gauge: In stitch patt (tr flo), 4"/10 cm should equal:
Small: 16 sts and 5½ rows = 4"/10cm using H-8/5mm hook in stitch patt (tr flo)
Medium: 14 sts and 4¾ rows = 4"/10cm using J-9/6mm hook in stitch patt (tr flo)
Large: 13 sts and 4½ rows = 4"/10cm using K-10½ / 6.5mm hook in stitch patt (tr flo)

Notions: Tapestry needle

CROCHET STITCHES USED: SL ST (CROCHET), SC, HDC, DC, TR, FLO, BLO

Sl st: Slip crochet hook into st, yo, draw loop through st and through loop on hook.

Sc (single crochet): Insert hook in stitch. YO hook. Pull yarn through stitch. YO hook. Pull yarn through 2 loops on hook (one single crochet made).

Hdc (half double crochet): YO hook. Insert hook in the next stitch to be worked. YO hook. Pull yarn through stitch. YO hook. Pull yarn through all 3 loops on hook (one half double crochet made).

Dc (double crochet): YO hook, insert hook in the next stitch to be worked, YO hook, draw through stitch, YO hook, draw through first 2 loops on hook, YO hook, draw through rem 2 loops on hook.

Tr (treble crochet): YO twice, insert hook in the next stitch to be worked, YO, draw yarn through stitch—3 loops on hook, YO, draw through first 2 loops on hook, YO, draw through first 2 loops on hook, YO, draw through rem 2 loops on hook.

Flo (front loop only): Work into the front loop only of the stitch, regardless of whether the right or wrong side of work is facing.

Blo (back loop only): Work into the back loop only of the stitch, regardless of whether the right or wrong side of work is facing.

Granny Triangle (Make 1)

In each round the beginning ch 3 counts as 1 dc; the beginning ch 5 counts as 1 dc + 2 ch.

With A, ch 4, sl st in first ch (to form a ring).

Round 1: Ch 3 (counts as first dc), work 2 dc in ring, (ch 2, 3 dc in ring) twice, ch 2, sl st to 3rd ch of beginning ch 3.

Round 2: Ch 5 (counts as 1 dc + 2 ch), (sk next 3 dc, work 3 dc in next space, ch 2, work 3 dc in same space as prev 3 dc, ch 2] twice, sk next 3 dc, 3 dc in next space, ch 2, 2 dc in same space as prev 3 dc, sl st to 3rd ch of beginning ch 5. Join B, do not cut A.

Round 3: With B, ch 3 (counts as first dc), 2 dc in next space, [ch 2, (3 dc, ch 2, 3 dc) in next space, ch 2, 3 dc in next space) twice, ch 2, (3 dc, ch 2, 3 dc) in next space, end round with ch 2 and sl st to 3rd ch of beginning ch 3.

Round 4: Ch 5, 3 dc in next space, [ch 2, (3 dc, ch 2, 3 dc) in next space, (ch 2, 3 dc in next space) twice] twice, ch 2, (3 dc, ch 2, 3dc) in next space, ch 2, 2 dc in next space, end with a sl st to 3rd ch of beginning ch 3. Break B.

Round 5: Gently draw A up from where it rests and ch 3 (counts as 1 dc), 2 dc in space, [ch 2, 3 dc in next space, ch 2, (3 dc, ch 2, 3 dc) in next space, (ch 2, 3 dc in next space) twice] twice, ch 2, 3 dc in next space, ch 2, (3 dc, ch 2, 3 dc) in next space, ch 2, 3 dc in next space, end round with ch 2, sl st to 3rd ch of beginning ch 3.

For Sizes Small and Large: Cut yarn here; triangle is finished and should measure approx 6¼"/16cm on each side.

Round 6 (Medium only): Ch 5, 3 dc in next space, (ch 2, 3 dc in next space, ch 2, [3 dc, ch 2, 3 dc] in next space, [ch 2, 3 dc in next space] 3 times) twice, ch 2, 3 dc in next space, ch 2, (3 dc, ch 2, 3 dc) in next space, ch 2, 3 dc in next space, ch 2, 2 dc in next space, sl st to 3rd ch of beginning ch 3. Tie off and break yarn; triangle should measure approx 6¾"/17cm on each side.

Top Section

You will now be working flat along 2 sides of granny triangle, turning work at end of each row and working in front loop only (flo) of each st.

Size Medium
Row 1: Attach Yarn A to second ch of any corner, ch 4 (counts as first tr), work 15 tr flo, 5 dc flo, 5 hdc flo, 4 sc flo (you are now at second corner of the triangle), 4 sc flo, 5 hdc flo, 5 dc flo, 16 tr flo—60 sts. Turn.

Rows 2–10: Ch 4, 15 tr flo, 5 dc flo, 5 hdc flo, 8 sc flo, 5 hdc flo, 5 dc flo, 16 tr flo—60 sts.

Turn and break Yarn A.

Sizes Small and Large
Row 1: Attach Yarn A to second ch of any corner, ch 4 (counts as first tr), 12 tr flo, 4 dc flo, 4 hdc flo, 4 sc flo (you are now at second corner of the triangle), 4 sc flo, 4 hdc flo, 4 dc flo, 13 tr flo—50 st. Turn.

Rows 2–8: Ch 4, 12 tr fl, 4 dc flo, 4 hdc flo, 8 sc flo, 4 hdc flo, 4 dc flo, 13 tr flo—50 sts.

Turn and break Yarn A.

Contrasting Seam and Crown

Fold the hat in half so that the fold goes right though the granny triangle and the rows are evenly spaced on each side. Join Yarn B along the narrowest, sc section (top of hat) and join both sides by working in sc, but insert hook into both layers of fabric. Sc both edges together (crocheting over any loose ends as you work) until you reach the bottom of hat, the wide tr section. Do not cut yarn.

Bottom Band

With right side of work facing you, work in sc blo along the edges of the trs and the third side of the granny triangle, around the entire circumference of the hat bottom as follows:

Ch 1, 3 sc along each tr and ch 4 space, 1 sc in each st from granny triangle, 3 sc along each tr and ch 4 space, join round with sl st—73 (92) sc. Try the hat on and if the fit feels too loose or too tight, this is the point to adjust the number of sc around the hat bottom. Work 2 (3, 2) rounds in sc flo.

Optional Earflaps

Size Medium

Right Earflap: Sk 16 sc, join Yarn A in next sc, sk 3 sc and work 8 tr in next st, sk 3 sc, sl st in next st. Tie off and cut Yarn A.

Left Earflap: Sk 42 sc, join Yarn A in next sc, sk 3 sc and work 8 tr in next st, sk 3 sc, sl st in next st. Tie off and cut Yarn A.

Sizes Small and Large

Right Earflap: Sk 11 sc, join Yarn A in next sc, sk 3 sc and work 8 tr in next st, sk 3 sc, sl st in next st. Tie off and cut Yarn A.

Left Earflap: Sk 3 sc, join Yarn A in next sc, sk 3 sc and work 8 tr in next st, sk 3 sc, sl st in next st. Tie off and cut Yarn A.

All Sizes

Work one last row of sc blo with Yarn B around bottom of hat, including earflaps. Weave in ends and block.

0006

Two-Toned Baby Hat
Katie Ahlquist

Deceptively simple, the technique for creating this adorable hat in the round will twist the brain at first, then become second nature!

Sizes: Baby (Child, Teen, Adult)
Finished Meas: To fit head size approx 14 (16, 18 ½, 21)"/35.5 (40.5, 47, 53.5)cm
Sample Size: Baby
Skill Level: K 2 Easy

Fiber: Plymouth Dreambaby DK (183yds/167m, 1.75oz/50gr) per skein
    Yarn A - Pink 126, 1 ball
    Yarn B - Gray 125, 1 ball
    (www.plymouthyarn.com)

Needles: Size US 6/4mm, 16"/40.5cm long circular needle for Baby size or size needed to achieve gauge. Use size US 7/4.5mm needle for Child size; size US 8/5mm for Teen size; size US 9/5.5mm for Adult size, going up a needle size for each larger size hat.

Notions: 3 stitch markers in 3 different colors, double-pointed needles (dpn) for I-cord, tapestry needle

Gauge: 24 (21, 18, 16) sts = 4"/10cm using size US 6/4mm 16"/40.5cm long circular needle

SPECIAL TECHNIQUES

Kitchener Stitch

To prepare, break yarn, leaving a tail 3 times the length of the seam; thread tail through a tapestry needle. Place pieces to be joined with WS together and hold both needles in the left hand. Move the stitches toward the points to make manipulation easier.

1. FRONT NEEDLE: Draw the tail through the 1st stitch on the front needle as if to purl, but do not slip stitch off needle.

2. BACK NEEDLE: Draw yarn through the 1st stitch on the back needle as if to knit, but do not slip stitch off needle.

3. FRONT NEEDLE: Draw tail through the 1st stitch on the front needle as if to knit, slip stitch off needle.

4. FRONT NEEDLE: Draw tail through the 2nd stitch on the front needle as if to purl, do not slip stitch off needle.

5. BACK NEEDLE: Draw tail through the 1st stitch on the back needle as if to purl, slip stitch off needle.

6. BACK NEEDLE: Draw tail through the 2nd

stitch on the back needle as if to knit, do not slip stitch off of needle.

Rep steps 3–6 until all stitches are joined. It is important to maintain an even tension in each stitch as you work because this method can be difficult to undo.

Setup

With A and circular needle, CO 84 sts. Join and place marker "A" (MA) to note start of round. K41, place marker "B" (MB) to note color change. K1, inc into next st (knit into front and back of st), place marker "C" (MC), k to end of round.

Colorwork Steps

1. Slip MA. Bring Color B from under Color A and with Color B knit to MB.

2. Slip MB, K2tog-L, TURN. Wrap the yarn over the top of the right needle to the back and under to the front, forming a YO. Purl 1, slip marker, purl to MA.

3. Slip MA. Bring Color A from under Color B and with Color A, purl to MC.

4. Slip MC, p2tog. TURN. YO, k1, slip MC, knit to MA.

Rep steps 1–4 until hat, unrolled, measures 6¼ (7, 8 ¼, 9 ½)"/16 (18, 21, 24)cm or desired depth, ending with step 4. Remove markers B and C in the last repetition, and do not work a YO.

You are at MA. Slip marker, bring Color B from under Color A, with Color B k18. Using a dpn, knit 6 sts from left needle. Slide these sts to the right tip of the dpn. Take a second dpn and work I-cord over these 6 sts for 6¼ (7, 8¼, 9½)"/16 (18, 21, 24)cm. K2tog 3 times, cut yarn, and thread it through the 3 rem sts. With a darning needle draw the tail down inside the I-cord to conceal it.

Take up your circular needle where you left it at the base of the Color B I-cord. Slip sts from right needle to left needle until you reach Color A, remove marker. Turn so WS is facing.

Using Color A, purl 18 sts. Slip next 6 sts onto a dpn. Turn so RS is facing. Slide the 6 sts to the right tip of the dpn. Take a second dpn, and bring the yarn behind the sts to the right-most one, pulling firmly after working the first st, and work I-cord, same as for the I-cord you worked in Color B.

The remaining sts are divided in half, still on your circular needle. If desired, transfer them to dpns in preparation to work Kitchener stitch. With the Color A half on the right, join a length of Color A near the right-most stitch on the back needle.

Finishing

Use Kitchener Stitch to join the top of the hat. When you come to the color transition, join a length of Color B to match that half. Leave a generous tail at the beginning and end of your seam so you can use it to sew up the gap or tighten loose stitches near the base of the I-cords. Weave in ends on the wrong side of the hat and block; tie I-cords in a square knot (not too tight!)

0007

Hat for Warm Necks

Ellen M. Silva

This hat uses the Channel cast-on and welt construction reminiscent of techniques used on classic Scottish ganseys. The cast-on forms a decorative and durable edge and the welted band provides a snug but comfortable fit with a longer neck welt for extra warmth. Designs formed of knit and purl stitches and a few small cables are knit from charts and the crown is decreased along six seed stitch faux seams, again recalling the faux seams used in authentic ganseys.

Size: One Size
Finished Meas: To fit head size 23"/58.5cm
Skill Level: K 3 Intermediate

Fiber: Green Mountain Spinnery, Sylvan Spirit (180yds/164m, 2oz/57gr) per skein
    Color - Antique Brass, 2 balls

Needles: Size US 4/3.5mm, 16"/40.5cm long circular and double-pointed needles (dpns)

Notions: One additional circular needle of any length, one additional double-pointed needle US size 4/3.5mm or smaller gauge for use in transferring stitches, stitch markers

Gauge: 22 sts and 34 rows = 4"/10cm in St st using size US 4/3.5mm, 16"/40.5cm circular needle or size needed to achieve gauge

SPECIAL TECHNIQUES

Channel Cast-On: Fold the yarn back on itself, resulting in a doubled yarn roughly as long in inches as the number of stitches to be cast on.

Close to the cut end of the yarn, form a slipknot over the needle, as for a long-tail cast-on. This slipknot is your first cast-on stitch. There will be three strands, one attached to the yarn ball (strand A) and two in a loop, which should be handled as one unit (strand B).

Arrange the yarn similar to a long-tail cast-on, with strand A passing over the index finger and strand(s) B wrapped around the thumb—BUT wrap strand B twice clockwise around thumb.

With the needle tip, go over the top of strand A and catch the yarn, then bring the tip up through both loops of strand(s) B and catch strand A again, pulling it through the loops around the thumb.

Drop the loops off the thumb and gently snug the resulting knot up below the cast-on. This manipulation results in two cast-on stitches with a decorative knot below.

Continue in this manner until a sufficient number of stitches have been cast-on.

A characteristic of this type of cast-on is that if your slipknot uses both strands of the doubled yarn, you will always end up with an even number of stitches.

If you need an odd number of stitches, simply knit two together on the first round.

Front Welt

Using the Channel Cast-On (or your preferred method), CO 73 sts.

Row 1 (WS): Inc 1 st (k1fb) in first st, knit across until 2 sts rem, k1fb, k1.

Row 2 (RS): Knit across.

Rep rows 1–2 three more times—81 sts total. Knit 2 rows even. Break working yarn, leaving several inches to weave in later. Transfer sts to spare circular needle of any smaller size or to a piece of waste yarn and set aside.

Back Welt

CO 63 sts. Knit as for front welt, but after the inc rows, knit even for approx 2"/5cm, ending on RS (after an even row)—71 sts. Do not break yarn.

You will now set up the welts for joining and to begin knitting the crown. There are 71 sts of the back welt on your project needle (Needle A). Transfer 14 sts from the end of the back welt attached to the working yarn to a spare circular or dpn (Needle B). Position the needle holding the front welt (Needle C) in front of Needle B. The broken yarn from the front welt on Needle C should be at the far end, to the left. Place marker. Transfer 1 st from Needle B to Needle A. Transfer 1 st from Needle C to Needle A. Rep this transfer, alternately transferring sts from Needle B, then C, until all of the sts from Needle B have been transferred back to Needle A. You have overlapped the welt by 14 sts.

Continue transferring sts from Needle C to Needle A until you have 14 sts rem on Needle C. Place marker. Bring the other end of Needle A around to meet the end that has been picking up sts from Needle C, positioning it behind Needle C and taking care not to twist the welts (both welts should be hanging straight down). Rep the alternating transfer of sts, 1 st from Needle A, then 1 st from Needle C, until all sts are transferred and the welts are joined in a circle.

You now have the beg of the crown of your hat. The front welt is lapped over the back welt by 14 sts on each side. On the next round you will knit the front welt and back welt sts together, ending with a total of 124 sts, as follows:

Knit around the tube to the first marker, 1 st from back welt remains before front welt sts beg. K2tog 14 times, joining the 28 overlapped sts into 14 single sts. Continue knitting across the front welt until you reach the second marker. This time the front welt is covering the point of overlap. Again, k2tog 14 times to join the front and back welt sts. Place marker to indicate beg of round. You should end with 124 sts on your needle, joined in a round.

Crown

The hat crown is composed of a series of charted designs. First a band of Chart A is repeated around the circumference of the hat, followed by a purl ridge. This is followed by Charts B, C, B, D, E, F, G, F, E, and D, all placed in sequence around the crown, with chart G centered at the front of the hat. A divider ridge of purl sts is worked after the sequence of charts, and then the dec section to close the crown, using chart H, is worked.

Beg by working Chart A, starting immediately after completing your joining round. Rep Chart A for a total of 31 times, resulting in a series of arrowheads chasing themselves around the crown of your hat.

Purl 2 rounds.

Beg working the gansey designs from Charts B through G in the following sequence:

B C B D E F G F E D

Chart B: This 2-row chart is repeated vertically as needed to fill the space between the taller charts.

Chart C: Space for initials or other personalization. Fill the blank area as you wish.

Chart D: Stacked filled and hollow diamonds.

Chart E: Another simple 2-row filler chart.

Chart F: A 2-st cable bordered by purl stitches. Rep this 4-row chart vertically to fill space between taller charts.

Chart G: Tree of Life.

After completing the 32 row charts, purl 1 round, then work 1 round as foll: P6, (p2tog, p10) 9 times, p2tog, p to end—114 sts. Slip marker and start Chart H, repeating 6 times around the crown. The double dec at the beg of the fifth rep of the chart should line up with the center line of the Tree of Life. Continue with Chart H, switching to dpns as needed.

At the end of Chart H, 6 sts rem. Break your working yarn and thread through these sts, cinching tightly and weaving end in. Weave

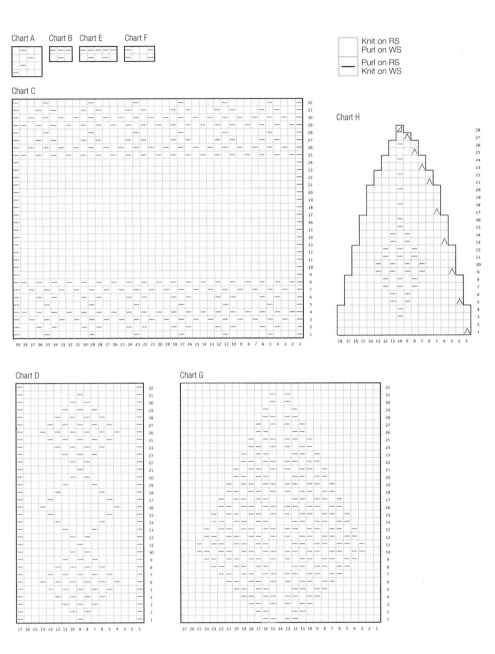

Hat for Warm Necks Stitch Charts

remaining edges in. Block by soaking in warm water, adding a wool wash if desired. Squeeze water gently from hat and roll in a towel for 15 minutes, then shape hat over a hat form, rolled towel, or balloon, being careful not to stretch the hat excessively. For perfect shape, block it on your head and wear until dry for a perfect fit.

Igloo
Woolly Wormhead

This easy-to-knit hat has amazing WOW appeal! It is a great hat for anyone who needs a warm place to put her ponytail!

Sizes: Small (Medium, Large)
Finished Meas: To fit head size 19¼ (20¼, 21¾)"/49 (51.5, 55)cm
Sample Size: Medium
Skill Level: K 2 Easy

Fiber: Frog Tree Alpaca Worsted (174yds/160m, 3.5oz/100gr) per skein
　　　Color - Green 41, 1 ball

Needles: Size US 7/4.5mm, 16"/40.5cm long circular and double-pointed needles (dpns) or size needed to achieve gauge

Notions: Stitch markers, tapestry needle

Gauge: 18 sts and 24 rows = 4"/10cm in St st using size US 7/4.5mm 16"/40.5cm long circular needle

Crown
With dpns, CO 7 sts.

Preparation Row: *Kfb, rep to end of round—14 sts. Join work, being careful not to twist the sts; place marker to note start of round.

Round 1: *K1, M1, k1; rep from * to end of round—21 sts.

Round 2: *K1, M1, k2; rep from * to end of round—28 sts.

Round 3: *K1, M1, k3; rep from * to end of round—35 sts.

Round 4: *K1, M1, k4; rep from * to end of round—42 sts.

Round 5: *K1, M1, k5; rep from * to end of round—49 sts.

Round 6: *K1, M1, k6; rep from * to end of round—56 sts.

Round 7: *K1, M1, k7; rep from * to end of round—63 sts.

Round 8: *K1, M1, k8; rep from * to end of round—70 sts.

Continue in this manner, increasing 7 sts per round until there are 84 (91, 98) sts on the needle, switching to circular needle if you wish.

Work 3 (4, 5) rounds of St st with no increasing.

Tunnel Shaping (worked back and forth)
Row 1 (RS): BO 2 sts, knit to end.

Row 2 (WS): BO 2 sts, purl to end.

Row 3: K2tog-R, knit to last 2 sts, K2tog-R.

Row 4: Purl all sts.

Row 5: K2tog-R, knit to last 2sts, K2tog-R.

Row 6: Purl all sts.

Row 7: Kfb, knit to last st, kfb.

Row 8: Purl all sts.

Row 9: Kfb, knit to last st, kfb.

Row 10: Purl to end, then CO 2 sts, turn.

Row 11: Knit to end, then CO 2 sts.

Rejoin work to continue knitting in the round.

Body
Work in St st (knit all sts) in the round until work measures 5¼ (5¾, 6¼)"/13 (14.5, 16)cm from tip of crown.

Next Round: K82 (91, 96), K2tog-R 1 (0, 1) times—83 (91, 97) sts.

Moss Stitch Band
Round 1: K1, *p1, k1; rep from * to end.

Round 2: P1, *k1, p1; rep from * to end.

Work Moss St band for approximately 1½"/3.75cm

Earflaps (work same for both)
Next Round: BO 12 (13, 13) sts, work 15 (17, 19) sts in pattern as est (1st earflap), BO 30 (31, 32) sts, work 15 (17, 19) sts in pattern as est (2nd earflap), BO 11 (13, 14) sts.

With RS of work facing, rejoin yarn to 1st earflap and work as follows:

Row 1 (RS): K2tog-L, work in pattern as est to last 2 sts, K2tog-R.

Row 2 (WS): Work in pattern as est (no decrease).

Rep above 2 rows until 3 sts rem. At this point you can either BO these sts for a regular earflap finish, or work these sts in Moss St for 9½"/23.5cm (or desired length) to create a tie.

Tunnel
With RS of work facing, pick up and k4 sts along the base of the tunnel "hole" (where you CO the extra sts to rejoin in the round), 7 sts up the left side of the tunnel, 4 sts across the top (where you bound off), and 7 sts down the right side—22 sts.

　　Work in Moss St in the round until tunnel measures 1½"/3.75cm (or desired length). BO loosely.

Finishing
Weave in all ends. Block lightly to allow the increase lines to settle.

0009

Pointy Striped Color

Tori Seierstad, Torirot Design

This beautiful stranded hat is a perfect project to play with the colors in your stash. In a new take on traditional colorwork, this pattern has some rows where three colors are worked together.

Sizes: Small (Large)
Finished Meas: To fit head size 17½ (20¼)"/45 (52)cm
Hat Depth: 9 3/4 (11 3/4")/25 (30) cm
Sample Size: Small
Skill Level: K 3 Intermediate

Fiber: Stash fingering weight yarn, approx 50yds/45m per color

  Yarn A - Burgundy
  Yarn B - Green
  Yarn C - Dark Red
  Yarn D - Medium Red
  Yarn E - Purple
  Yarn F - Light Orange
  Yarn G - Light Red
  Yarn H - Brownish Red

Needles: For Small: Sizes US 0/2mm and US 1/2.5mm 16"/40.5cm long circular or double-pointed needles (dpns); for Large: sizes US 3/3.25mm and US 4/3.5mm 16"/40.5cm long circular or double-pointed needles; or size needed to achieve gauge

Notions: Tapestry needle, stitch marker, optional crochet hook

Gauge: Small: 28 sts and 37 rows = 4"/10cm in stranded pattern using sizes US 0/2mm and US 1/2.5mm 16"/40.5cm circular needles
  Large: 23 sts and 29 rows = 4"/10 cm in stranded pattern using sizes US 3/3.25mm and US 4/3.5mm 16"/40.5cm circular needles

Notes: *The suggested colors are yarns Tori had on hand from her stash for the red hat, but these colors can be changed or adapted to suit your own taste.*
  The first star pattern (Chart A) involves some rounds with three colors. If you prefer only two colors at a time, you can choose to drop the third color from these rounds and use a currently working color.
  The four colorwork charts are worked in sequence (A, B, C, and D for the earflaps) from the bottom of each chart (row 1) to the top. Row numbers are listed every 4th row.
  There will be decreases between Charts A and B, or in specific rows of Chart C as listed below. As you work these there will be places in Chart C where the patterns will not line up in subsequent rows.

Hem

With A and smaller circular needle, CO 128 sts. Place marker and join in the round. Work around in St st (knit every round) for 15 rounds. Purl 1 round (folding ridge).
  Switch to larger needles and beginning with row 1, rep Chart A 8 times around all sts for a total of 28 rows.
  After Chart A work 1 round in A, dec 2 sts in round—126 sts.
  Beginning with row 1, rep Chart B 14 times around all sts for a total of 10 rows.
  Beginning with row 1, work Chart C, making the decs as foll:

Round 4: *K5, k2tog-R; rep from * to end of round—108 sts.

Round 8: *K7, k2tog-R; rep from * to end of round—96 sts.

Round 14: *K6, k2tog-R; rep from * to end of round—84 sts.

Round 20: *K5, k2tog-R; rep from * to end of round—72 sts.

Round 24: *K4, k2tog-R; rep from * to end of round—60 sts.

Round 32: *K3, k2tog-R; rep from * to end of round—48 sts.

Round 38: *K2, k2tog-R; rep from * to end of round—36 sts.

Round 44: *K1, k2tog-R; rep from * to end of round—24 sts.

Round 48: *K2tog-R; rep from * to end of round—12 sts.

Round 52: *K2tog-R; rep from * to end of round—6 sts.

Note: *As the decs are worked the patterns will not line up in subsequent rows. This is fine, and is expected.*

Continue working in Chart C, dec'ing as directed. Switch to dpns when the hat gets too small for circular needle. With tapestry needle, draw yarn tightly through rem 6 sts. Weave in end, but don't cut the yarn, as you will use this to fasten the pom-pom.

Pom-Pom: Take all the different yarns, wrap them around your fingers (or something else measuring approx 3"/8cm) 6–8 times. Knot tightly approx ¾"/2cm from one end and sew it to the hat, making sure you fasten it well. Cut the yarn at the other end after the pom-pom is securely attached.

Finishing

Weave in all loose ends. Fold and sew up hem.

Left Earflap: Measure 2½ (3)"/6 (7)cm from the center back point of hat on the left side. With one dpn, pick up 22 sts from front of the purled sts (folding ridge), and with another dpn pick up 22 sts from the back of the same sts. Move the sts onto four dpns. Start working in the round (the first rounds are a little tricky). Work according to Chart D, starting with the RS toward you. The chart will be repeated once for the front and once for the back side of earflap.

Right Earflap: Work as for left, picking up sts from the folding ridge 2½ (3)"/6 (7)cm from the center back point of hat on the right side.

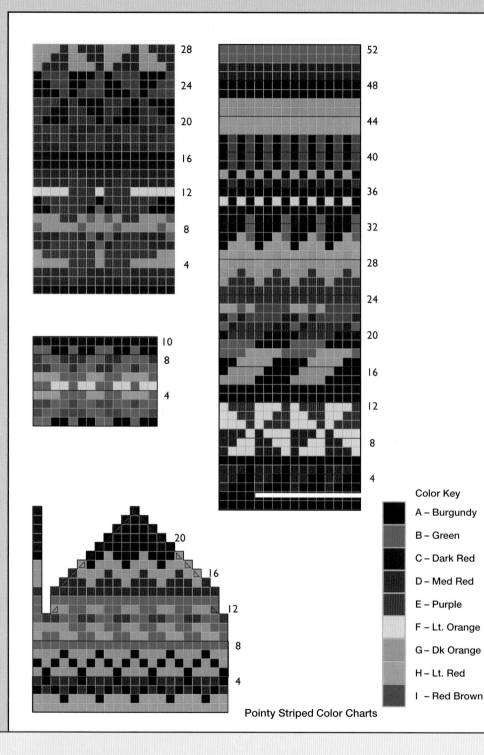

28
24
20
16
12
8
4

52
48
44
40
36
32
28
24
20
16
12
8
4

10
8
4

20
16
12
8
4

Color Key

A – Burgundy

B – Green

C – Dark Red

D – Med Red

E – Purple

F – Lt. Orange

G – Dk Orange

H – Lt. Red

I – Red Brown

Pointy Striped Color Charts

Ties

Option 1 (Crochet): With crochet hook, draw yarn through rem 4 sts. Chain until the cord measures desired length. Turn, work 1 sc into each chain until you are back up to the earflap. Weave in end.

Option 2 (I-cord): Move the rem 4 sts onto one dpn. K2tog, k2—3 sts rem on needle. Work an I-cord to desired length. Bind off. Weave in end.

Option 3 (Braid): Leave 8–10"/20–25cm tails of the last 6 colors used in the earflap. Draw yarn of the last color through rem 4 sts. Join two and two colors, and make a tight braid to your desired length.

0010

Cabled Tie Topper

Kathryn L. Oates, Tot Toppers

Here is an adorable baby hat knit in the round from the bottom up combining Fair Isle technique, cabling, and texture. The cap is topped with a knotted tie.

Notes: When changing colors in a row, loosely carry unused color along WS of work to prevent puckering. In crown-shaping section, change to double-pointed needles when sts do not slide easily around circular needle.

Sizes: 3 months (6 months, 1 year, 2 years, 3 years)
Finished Meas: To fit head sizes 13 (15, 17, 18½, 20)"/33.3 (38.5, 43.6, 47.4, 51.3)cm
Sample Size: 13"/33.3cm
Skill Level: K 3 Intermediate

Fiber: Debbie Bliss Stella (91yds/83m, 1.75oz/50gr) per skein
Yarn A - Sunflower 16, 1 ball
Yarn B - Teal 14, 1 ball

Needles: Size US 7/4.5mm 16"/40.5cm long circular needle and double-pointed needles (dpns) or size needed to achieve gauge

Notions: Tapestry needle, cable needle (cn), stitch marker

Gauge: 19 sts and 24 rows = 4"/10cm in St st on size US 7/4.5mm 16"/40.5cm long circular needle

SPECIAL TECHNIQUE

C4L (aka C4F): *Cable 4 sts with Left twist: Slip 2 sts to cn, k2 sts, bring slipped sts to front of work and knit them.*

Band

With circular needle and A, CO 63 (72, 81, 90, 99) sts. Place marker and join in the round, being careful not to twist work. Work in St st (knit every round) until piece measures 1"/2.5cm from CO edge.

Establish Cable Pattern

Preparation Round: *With B, k1; with A, k2; with B, k4; with A, k2; rep from * to end of round.

Beg with stitch 1, round 1 of chart, work rounds 1–4 in Cable Patt as est. Rep these four rounds 3 (4, 5, 6, 7) more times, end with rep round 1 of Cable Tie Topper Color/Cable Chart.

Crown Shaping

Continuing chart as est, work rounds 5–11, dec'ing in rounds 5, 6, 8, and 10 where noted. Rep round 11 once more, then cut yarn B and continue last several rounds with A only.

Next Round: *K2, k2tog; rep from * to end of round.

Next Round: *K1, k2tog; rep from * to end of round.

Remove st marker and k2tog until only 5 sts rem.

Cord Tip

Work in I-cord for 4"/10cm.

BO, cut yarn, and weave through rem st. Secure, weaving in yarn tail.

Finishing

Weave in all loose ends. Steam block hat lightly. Tie the I-cord on top of the hat into a knot, sliding the knot so that it is toward the base of the hat. I prefer my knot on the loose side. The I-cord should form a cute little sprout on top of the knot.

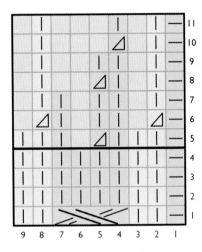

Preparation Round

Cabled Tie Topper Color / Cable Chart

Contributors

~A~

M Kathryn Adkins, USA
mkathrynadkins@gmail.com
www.grammykate.blogspot.com;
www.ravelry.com/people/
granmakate
0245

Katie Ahlquist, USA
kt_ahlquist@yahoo.com
www.sparkledesign.net/fidget
0006, 0110, 0149, 0150, 0212

Yvonne Allen, USA
allenyc@yahoo.com
0014, 0061, 0065, 0087, 0096,
0382, 0384, 0399, 0417, 0436,
0565, 0567, 0639, 0641, 0739,
0788, 0809

Emily Allison, Stitches 4 Bitches,
USA
www.stitches4bitches.etsy.com
0396, 0418

Ruth Altheim, USA
ruthaltheim@yahoo.com
www.digibabeknits.blogspot.com
0638

Irene Armock, USA
0995

~B~

Alicia McLemore Bal, USA
aliciabal@mac.com
www.knittnmama.blogspot.com
0442

Lee Ann Balazuc, Canada
lee-ann@balazuc.net
www.fuzzylogicknits.com
0731

Sarah-Marie Belcastro, USA
smbelcas@toroidalsnark.net
www.toroidalsnark.net
0416

**Sandra Benward, Camellia City
Stockin'ettes Knit Guild**, USA
Slbenward@comcast.net
0218, 0279, 0303, 0354, 0587,
0698, 0699

**Michele Lee Bernstein,
PDXKnitterati**, USA
PDXKnitterati@comcast.net
www.pdxknitterati.com
0710, 0727, 0773, 0938

**Marci Blank, Th'Red Head
Designs**, USA
thred_head@yahoo.com
www.thredhead.com
0028, 0079, 0101, 0108, 0129,
0194, 0200, 0219, 0300, 0347,
0357, 0440, 0466, 0732

Anne Blayney, Canada
anne.blayney@gmail.com
www.anniebeeknits.wordpress.com
0029, 0152, 0162, 0163, 0235,
0283, 0286, 0311, 0483, 0497,
0586, 0600, 0753

Toni Blye, It's Curious, USA
toni@itscurious.com
www.itscurious.com
0421, 0430, 0618, 0623, 0707

Lexi Boeger, USA
www.pluckyfluff.com
0076, 0160, 0323, 0397, 0420,
0427, 0876

Sam Boice, Lorna's Laces, USA
yarn@lornaslaces.net
www.lornaslaces.net
0046, 0151, 0185, 0204, 0438,
0451

Isabelle Boutin, Canada
boutinisabelle@hotmail.com
www.isanou.wordpress.com
0481, 0906

Anne E. P. Boyer, USA
Macred1@verizon.net
www.witwithknit.wordpress.com
0815, 0881, 0887, 0902, 0931

Deb Boyken, Knitting Scholar,
USA
deb@knittingscholar.com
www.knittingscholar.com
0409

Ruth Bramley, UK
ruth@bramleyfamilyorg.uk
0091, 0413, 0419

Heather Broadhurst, USA
hjnb@boddame.net
0984

**Joelle Burbank, Adirondack
Knits**, USA
joelle.burbank@gmail.com
www.adirondackknits.com
0782

Catherine Bursell, UK
cjm@2p2trust.org
www.bluecowmoo.blogspot.com
0959

Gunilla Buzzelli, Canada
gunillabuzzelli@hotmail.com
0118, 0132, 0138, 0140

~C~

**Charisa Martin Cairn,
K1P1Design1**, USA
Charisa@k1p1design1.com
www.k1p1design1.com
0231, 0310, 0751

Sue Caldwell, Lovelyarns, USA
lovelyarns@verizon.net
www.lovelyarns.com
0153, 0823

Beth Callahan, USA
beth.callahan@synergex.com
www.topfrog.blogspot.com
0220, 0254

Elizabeth Carls, USA
elizabeth.c.carls@gmail.com
www.elizabethcarls.com
0036, 0048, 0106, 0501

**Suzanne Carter-Jackson, Zero
Cattle**, Canada
suzannecarterjackson@gmail.com
www.reformedurbanist.com
0676, 0752, 0759

Jessica Cheney, USA
jessicaknits@gmail.com
063, 0100, 0605, 0606

ChezPlum, France
sylvie@chezplum.com
www.chezplum.com
0005, 0011, 0015, 0025, 0026,
0053, 0155, 0178, 0179, 0193,
0297, 0405, 0446, 0448, 0518,
0522, 0848, 0879, 0892, 0942,
0955

**Jennifer J. Cirka, Jaybird
Designs**, USA
jaybird@acsol.net
www.jaybird-designs.com
0798, 0829, 0844

Rachel "Ivy" Clarke, USA
ivy@archivy.net
www.archivy.net
0500

Freyalyn Close-Hainsworth, UK
freyalynn@yahoo.com
www.Freyalyn.etsy.com
0077, 0134

Constance M. Cole, Constance
Creations, Canada
cole.slaw@nf.sympatico.ca
0003, 0062, 0258, 0287, 0385,
0574, 0584, 0622, 0628, 0767,
0783, 0869

Caroline Conery, USA
cityfish4@myfairpoint.net
www.dipndip.blogspot.com
0304, 0308, 0309, 0340, 0343,
0355, 0377, 0378, 0380

Kathleen A. Conery, USA
coneryka@jmu.edu
www.dipndip.blogspot.com
0156, 0361, 0374, 0989, 0992

Marion Conery, USA
coneryfm@aol.com
0339

Laurel Coombs, Lobug Designs,
USA
knitskate@q.com
www.lobug.blogspot.com
0890

Cosette Cornelius-Bates,
CosyKnits (literally), USA
cosyknitsliterally@gmail.com
www.cosymakes.com
0161, 0166, 0172, 0182, 0276,
0277, 0290, 0657, 0659, 0693,
0760

Anne Crawford, Canada
annecrawford@shaw.ca
www.madlyoffinalldirections
.blogspot.com
0285, 0293, 0366, 0615, 0764,
0768

Brenda Cunningham, USA
kwbcunning@sbcglobel.net
0256, 0312, 0359, 0612

Mary Ann Cutler, Canada
cutlermac@cogeco.ca
www.cutlermac.wordpress.com
0078, 0109, 0139, 0141, 0145,
0472, 0576

~D~

Jasmine Davis, USA
jdavis@chatham.edu
www.dangerbee.etsy.com
0069, 0471

Kimberly Davis, USA
0386

Annette M. Davis-Dill, USA
amdill@jonesday.com
0545

Susan Dewey, Bee Berry Woods,
USA
susan@beeberrywoods.com
www.beeberrywoods.com
0484

Tabitha Dick Oyediran, Knits So
Divine, USA
tabithadick@yahoo.com
mypageofwonderfulknits.blogspot
.com
0038, 0610, 0613, 0614, 0778

Amy M. Duncan, Funckie Dunckie
Knits, USA
dunck8@funckiedunckie.com
www.funckiedunckie.com
0067

~E~

Edie Eckman, USA
www.edieeckman.com
0795, 0813, 0921, 0969, 0988

Lorraine Ehrlinger, Lorraine
Ehrlinger Designs, USA
lehrlinger@sbcglobal.net
0216, 0652, 0766

Lois Ellen, Lois Ellen Designs,
USA
mhansen@leopardco.com
www.loisellen.etsy.com
0327, 0353, 0373, 0478, 0480,
0712

Bonnie Esplie, USA
esplie@aol.com
0666

~F~

Tricia Fagley, random threads
designs, USA
fagley@carolina.rr.com
www.randomthreads.com
0027, 0044, 0288, 0321, 0572,
0672, 0691, 0709, 0849

Sarah Fay, Canada
iamsarah@rogers.com
www.sarah_iam.blogspot.com
0187, 0237, 0443, 0658, 0968

Galina Fedtchenko, USA
galinafed@hotmail.com
0192

Carol Feller, Stolen Stitches,
Ireland
carol@stolenstitches.com
www.stolenstitches.com
0684, 0814, 0816

Corrina Ferguson, PicnicKnits,
USA
corrina@picnicknits.com
www.picnicknits.com
0456, 0494, 0569

Kristi Founds, Kristi L Knits, USA
iweavetoo@yahoo.com
0013, 0047, 0074, 0296

Katya Frankel, UK
dkstf@hotmail.co.uk
www.bingeknitter.blogspot.com
0023, 0031, 0088, 0453, 0474,
0479, 0489, 0777

Bonnie Franz, USA
www.bonniefranzdesigns.com
0910, 0932, 0941

Marti Fuerst, USA
cundiffme@gmail.com
www.cyclicalcreativity.blogspot.com
0431

Mandy Furney, Canada
0189, 0412, 0790, 0864, 0865,
0873, 0948, 0980, 0987, 0997

~G~

Rebecca Ganzel, USA
rebecca.ganzel@gmail.com
0711

Stefanie Goodwin-Ritter, Lorna's
Laces, USA
yarn@lornaslaces.net
www.lornaslaces.net
0499, 0632

Louise Gordon, UK
louise@woolfish.co.uk
www.woolfish.co.uk
0080, 0081, 0089, 0188, 0222,
0503, 0508, 0510, 0515, 0521,
0524, 0528, 0540, 0791

Edda Lilja Guðmundsdóttir,
Snigla, Iceland
snigla@snigla.com
www.snigla.com
0407, 0514, 0535, 0548, 0637,
0820, 0824, 0850, 0908, 0917,
0960

~H~

ErickaJo Haddad, USA
Erickajo@gmail.com
www.armedwithpointysticks.com
0350

Janice M. Hamby, TwinSet
Designs, USA
Jan@twinset.us
www.twinset.us
0082, 0348, 0985

Connie Haney, Bee Happy
Designs, USA
KnitNut@carolina.rr.com
www.beehappydesigns.com
0923

Josi Hannon Madera, Art of
Crochet, USA
josi@iamintheloop.com
www.artofcrochet.com
0174, 0302, 0344, 0507, 0533,
0534, 0700, 0706, 0758

Maria Hanson, USA
Mariajh1@msn.com
www.passingdowncrazy.wordpress
.com
0796, 0822

Sharon Hanson, Knot-Cha-Cha™,
USA
sharon@knot-cha-cha.com
www.knot-cha-cha.blogspot.com
www.knotchacha.etsy.com
0376, 0781

Katie Harmon, PinkPolish Design,
USA
info@pinkpolishdesign.com
www.pinkpolishdesign.com
0097, 0588, 0650, 0714, 0826,
0835, 0836, 1000

Rebecca Harmon, Mountain Mist
Fiberworks, USA
fiberworks@mountain-mist.com
www.mountain-mist.com
0012, 0018, 0037, 0057, 0072,
0102, 0107, 0184, 0295, 0325,
0329, 0352, 0491, 0519, 0651,
0653, 0667, 0674, 0675, 0677,
0682, 0683, 0685, 0686, 0690,
0741, 0789

Marina Hayes, USA
marol101@yahoo.com
www.ravelry.com/projects/RedStitch
0647, 0805

Deborah Heinzle, Switzerland
dheinzle@gmx.ch
0223, 0337, 0387

Sherry Heit, USA
purrbark@aol.com
0017, 0905

Kim Helmick, USA
KHelmickphotography@frontiernet
.net
www.kshotz.blogspot.com
0490

Shanna C. Henk, USA
Shanna.Henk@yahoo.com
www.crafty-shanna.livejournal.com
0406, 0428

Catherine Henry, USA
cathyannhenry@mac.com
www.ravelry.com/people/CathyAnn
0597

Lizette Hopkins, Spin-Glitz, USA
lizette@spinglitz.com
www.spinglitz.com
0794, 0878

Gina House, Sleepy Eyes
Knitting, USA
gina.sleepyeyes@gmail.com
www.sleepyeyesknitting.blogspot
.com
0330, 0332, 0335, 0345, 0349,
0367, 0971

Margaret Hubert, USA
mhdesigner1@gmail.com
www.margarethubertoriginals.com
www.margaretshooksandneedles
.blogspot.com
0059, 0064, 0085, 0113, 0117,
0120, 0209, 0210, 0250, 0268,
0272, 0338, 0393, 0449, 0523,
0525, 0544, 0562, 0563, 0703,
0970

Carla Hukee, HUKEE, USA
carla@hukee.com
www.hukee.com
0742

~J~

Helen Jacobs-Grant, UK
myheartexposed@me.com
myheartexposed.co.uk
0744, 0769, 0806, 0903

Lisa Janowsky, USA
janglan@yahoo.com
lisaj@ravelry
0568, 0591

Lynn Johanna, Lady Willow
Designs, USA
ladywillow@earthlink.net
ladywillowtreehouse.wordpress
.com; http://community.webshots
.com/user/lady13willow
0392, 0402, 0531, 0532, 0536,
0537, 0550, 0553

Alexandra Johnson, Knitting
Nymph, Canada
alia.m.johnson@gmail.com
www.knittingnymph.etsy.com
0207, 0498, 0847, 0862, 0925,
0956, 0965

Jennifer Johnson, USA
0111, 0581, 0918

Shelley D. Jones, USA
Onegoodyarn@hotmail.com
0871

Harpa Jónsdóttir, Iceland
harpenstein@gmail.com;
harpajons@simnet.is
http://nopatterns.blogspot.com
0001, 0104, 0164, 0165, 0173,
0175, 0213, 0230

~K~

Mary Keenan, Canada
mary.keenan@rogers.com
www.marykeenanknits.com
0004, 0334

Brenda Marie Kelly,
Celticfireraven, USA
c4rent1@aol.com
celticfireraven.livejournal.com
0362, 0383, 0388

Michelle Kennedy, USA
YarnSoup@yahoo.com
0060, 0261, 0414, 0432, 0583,
0837, 0842, 0845, 0868, 0889,
0891, 0911, 0912, 0927, 0939,
0953

Kelly Klem, Klymyshyn Design,
USA
KellyKlem@cox.net
www.KlymyshynDesign.etsy.com
0589, 0660, 0828, 0840, 0915,
0998

Rachel Kluesner, Dyeabolical
Yarns, USA
stlrachelknits@gmail.com
www.dyeabolicalyarns.com
0040, 0437, 0715, 0725, 0756

Julie Kundhi, Kundhi.com, USA
jkundhi@kundhicreative.com
www.kundhi.com
0945

~L~

Melissa LaBarre, USA
knittingschooldropout@gmail.com
www.knittingschooldropout.com
0211, 0322, 0745, 0746

Janel Laidman, Rustling Leaf
Press, USA
mail@janellaidman.com
www.janellaidman.com
0070, 0073, 0793

Janine Le Cras, Guernseygal
Designs, UK
guernseygaldesigns@gogglemail
.com
guernseygal.typepad.com/
knitting_on_an_Island
0205

Kimberly Lewis, USA
wovenspun@gmail.com
0236

Dana Lorz, USA
danalorz@comcast.net
0604, 0631, 0896

Anne Kuo Lukito, USA
CraftyDiversions@gmail.com
www.CraftyDiversions.com
0035, 0055, 0066, 0071, 0103,
0116, 0124, 0159, 0203, 0206,
0271, 0716, 0724, 0737, 0748,
0749, 0762, 0772, 0774, 0996

Lucinda Luttgen, USA
leluttgen@earthlink.net
www.LucindaLuttgen.org
0331

~M~

A.M., USA
0364, 0370, 0465, 0475, 0477,
0681, 0722, 0723, 0729, 0872,
0975

Agnes Maderich, Hats by Agnes,
USA
amaderich@comcast.net
0093, 0119, 0143, 0148, 0195,
0217, 0227, 0251, 0265, 0266,
0317, 0468, 0485, 0596, 0608,
0780, 0838

Cynthia Marovich, Cynthia's Fine
Yarn & Gifts, USA
Cynthias702@aol.com
www.cynthiasyarn.citymax.com
0830

Margaret A. Martin, USA
martin@hitthenail.com
www.hittenail.com
0670

Laura Martos, Dizzy Blonde
Studios, USA
LauraMartos@sbcglobal.net
LauraMartos.wordpress.com
0246, 0394, 0496, 0907

AnneLena K. Mattison, USA
annelena@comcast.net
0305, 0486, 0694, 0696, 0728,
0967

Maria Maxwell, UK
0034, 0233, 0243, 0439, 0513,
0517, 0526, 0530, 0551, 0555,
0556

Amy McElwain, Amy McElwain's
Patterns, USA
mcelwainamy@yahoo.com
mcelwainamy.wordpress.com
0754

Sharon Menges, USA
Sharongoodfood@netzero.net
0135, 0144, 0167, 0168, 0196,
0208, 0400, 0634, 0636, 0817

Rebecca Mercier, USA
whimsicalknitting@comcast.net
whimsicalknitting.blogspot.com
0284, 0328, 0492, 0570, 0573,
0630, 0635, 0642, 0734, 0920,
0926

Lee Meredith, leethal, USA
leethalkoala@yahoo.com
www.lethal.net
0115, 0133, 0183, 0240, 0241,
0242, 0274, 0319, 0320, 0454,
0459, 0582, 0625, 0663, 0952

Lorna Miser, Lorna Miser
Designs, USA
lornaknits@yahoo.com
www.lornamiserdesigns.com
0249, 0291, 0292, 0356, 0358,
0365, 0713, 0841

Wanda Mitcham, USA
lancer32296@yahoo.com
0092, 0098, 0180, 0423

Annie Modesitt, USA
annie@modeknit.com
0122, 0123, 0127, 0128, 0130,
0170, 0201, 0410, 0529, 0575,
0577, 0580, 0592, 0594, 0598,
0602, 0607, 0643, 0708, 0730,
0874, 0963

Ruth R. Moline, 5elementknitr,
USA
Ruth@5elementknitr.com
www.5elementknitr.blogspot.com
0234, 0411, 0863

Terry Liann Morris, SailingKnitter
Liann Originals, USA
sailingknitter@yahoo.com
www.liannoriginals.com
0033, 0058, 0090, 0121, 0225,
0228, 0298, 0299, 0314, 0369,
0629, 0662, 0669, 0680, 0702,
0770, 0859, 0877, 0933, 0964,
0999

~N~

London Nelson, USA
London.nelson@gmail.com
www.myfriendlondon.com
0248, 0487, 0655, 0735

Kimberly Nico, USA
kimberly_nico@yahoo.com
0954

Kendra Nitta, USA
missknitta@gmail.com
www.missknitta.com
0197, 0593

Kathy North, Designs by KN, USA
kathy@designsbykn.com
www.designsbykn.com
0114, 0244, 0313, 0541, 0771,
0801

Celeste Nossiter, USA
Celeste.nossiter@pearson.com
0701

Kelli Nottingham,
www.savvyneedle.com, USA
kelli_nottingham@hotmail.com
www.savvyneedle.com
0198

Jane Nowakowski, USA
nowakows@rider.edu
0094, 0504, 0506, 0539, 0542,
0543, 0549, 0559, 0560, 0819,
0870

~O~

Kathryn L. Oates, Tot Toppers,
USA
TotToppers@gmail.com
www.TotToppersShop.com
0010, 0804, 0812, 0853, 0861,
0866, 0883, 0897, 0901, 0935,
0949, 0994

A. Greeley O'Connor, USA
agreeleyoconnor@mac.com
www.rideknitread.typepad.com
0360, 0473

Shannon Okey, knitgrrl.com, USA
admin@knitgrrl.com
www.knitgrrl.com
0083, 0086

Thea Orozco, USA
Atheame@yahoo.com
thatyarnstore.blogspot.com
0445

~P~

Jill Packard, USA
oboegoddess@gmail.com
0030, 0455, 0458, 0495, 0750

Rebecca Patterson, Artisan Yarns, USA
ripatterson@mac.com
www.artisan-yarns.com
0505, 0512, 0520, 0554, 0557, 0558

Lorna Pearman, Peargirl Knits, USA
knitpixie@msn.com
www.peargirlknits.blogspot.com
0922, 0991

Jessie J. Peissig, USA
jjpeis2003@yahoo.com
trouble-with-trebles.blogspot.com
0808

Tricia Pendergrass, USA
tpcougar@embarqmail.com
0281

Amy Pickard, UK
dyedinthewool.wordpress.com
0032, 0579, 0601

Amy Polcyn, USA
apolcyn@att.net
www.frottez.blogspot.com
0016

Maddie Pollis, USA
madeline5@aol.com
0252

Alasdair Post-Quinn, www.fallingblox.com, USA
fallingblox@gmail.com
www.fallingblox.com
0084, 0463, 0688, 0697, 0757, 0761

Christina Marie Potter, USA
Christina@christinamariepotter.com
www.christinamariepotter.com
0509

Mandy Powers, zigzagstitch, USA
oldredshed@gmail.com
www.myzigzagstitch.com
0002, 0169, 0171, 0202, 0255, 0275, 0301, 0726, 0779, 0893, 0936

Lisa Putman, USA
lisabai@gmail.com
0278, 0590

~R~

Jonelle Raffino, SWTC Collection, USA
jonelle@soysilk.com
0154, 0368, 0381, 0461, 0585, 0645, 0834, 0867, 0961

Sophia Raffino, SWTC Collection, USA
sophia@soysilk.com
0821

Becka Rahn, USA
beckarahn@gmail.com
www.beckarahn.com
0024

Becca Robbins, USA
Chopsaw.derby@gmail.com
0564, 0566

Louise Robert, Biscotte & Cie, Canada
biscotte_cie@hotmail.com
www.biscottecie.com
0856, 0880

Jeri Robinson-Lawrence, Flying Fibers, USA
jeri@flyingfibers.com
www.flyingfibers.com
0136, 0137

Beth Rodio, USA
Er71479@yahoo.com
www.myowntwosticks.com/blog
0039

Pam Pryshepa Ronan, digifigi, USA
pronan@usa.net
0099, 0181, 0511, 0561, 0611, 0616, 0619, 0640, 0644, 0648

~S~

Margit Sage, Fiber Fiend, USA
thefiend@fiberfiend.com
fiberfiend.com
0460, 0467, 0470, 0488, 0765

Cheryl Savage, Squirrels' Nest, USA
squirrelsnest6@yahoo.com
www.AKnittersChronicles.com
0324

Marie Segares, Underground Crafter, USA
marie@undergroundcrafter.com
www.undergroundcrafter.com
0289, 0444, 0516, 0527, 0546, 0547, 0552

Tanya L. Seidman, USA
0426

Tori Seierstad, Torirot Design, Norway
Torirot@gmail.com
torirotsstitches.blogspot.com
0009, 0214, 0282, 0656, 0704

Joanne Seiff, Canada
Joanne@joanneseiff.com
www.joanneseiff.com
0260, 0263, 0755, 0888

Cheryl Shores, USA
0843

Ellen M. Silva, TwinSet Designs, USA
e.silva@comcast.net
twinset.us
0007, 0199, 0441, 0665, 0692

Emily Simmons, Canada
0452, 0502, 0661, 0786

Sarah E. Sipe, USA
sesipe@gmail.com
durham_knits.dreamwidth.org
0747

Selina Siu, Canada
0415

Susie Slider, USA
susieg_wv2000@yahoo.com
0239, 0269, 0342

Jennifer Small, Blue Canary Creations, USA
jenrsmall@yahoo.com
bluecanary.typepad.com
0928

Dana K. Smith, USA
dana_smith_511@comcast.net
knitsmith-wordpurl.blogspot.com
0493, 0958

Kate JK Smith, USA
smith.kate@gmail.com
0904

Lies Spaink, The Netherlands
lies.typepad.com/knitting
0687, 0695, 0914, 0986

Jane Spaulding, CopperScaleDragon, USA
Copperscaledragon@gmail.com
copperscaledragon.blogspot.com
0105

Marie Stanley, That 80's Hat, USA
0538, 0978

Lisa Stanton, USA
lisalovs@comcast.net
0333, 0395, 0719

Andrea L. Stern, USA
andiandmarty@gmail.com
andibeads.blogspot.com
0389, 0390, 0391, 0398, 0403, 0404, 0408, 0425, 0433, 0435

Hester Sturrock, Hester Kate Knits, USA
0899, 0950

~T~

Erin Taylor Bell, USA
etaylorbell@gmail.com
0944

Michelle Tibbs & Elizabeth Cadieux, USA
mmtibbs@cyberonic.com
0799, 0807, 0810, 0827, 0832,
0857, 0882, 0884, 0885, 0886,
0895, 0898, 0900, 0916, 0919,
0924, 0930, 0946, 0966, 0973,
0974, 0976, 0977, 0981, 0982,
0983, 0990

Mari Tobita, USA
Maritobita@aol.com
0146, 0147

Angela Tong, USA
nyjeweler@hotmail.com
www.oiyi.blogspot.com
0259, 0429, 0846, 0851, 0854,
0860, 0913

Diana Troldahl, Otterwise Designs, USA
ottergal@comcast.net
otterwise.blogspot.com
0434, 0482

Sherria Tyler, Arcata Bay Llamas, USA
arcatabayllamas@msn.com
www.handspunyarn.com
0316

~V~

Zoë Valette, USA
Zoevalette@hotmail.com
Zoeknits.blogspot.com
0045, 0763

Carolyn Vance, USA
carovan@hickorytech.net
www.ravelry.com/designers/
carolyn-vance
0125, 0126, 0186, 0191, 0257,
0262, 0264, 0401, 0476, 0654,
0664, 0673, 0679, 0689, 0705,
0717, 0718, 0720, 0721, 0738,
0740, 0784, 0787, 0894, 0940,
0957

Rebecca Velasquez, USA
Rebecca@RebeccaVelasquez.com
www.RebeccaVelasquex.com
0620

Stephanie Voyer, Canada
birana007@yahoo.com
alamaille.blogspot.com
0341, 0678

~W~

Debby Ware, USA
wares@earthlink.net
www.debbyware.com
0797, 0825, 0855, 0875, 0979

Sarah E. White, knitting.about. com, USA
sewwriter@gmail.com
www.knitting.about.com
0221, 0270, 0372, 0422

Tina Whitmore for Knitwhits, USA
tina@knitwhits.com
www.knitwhits.com
0075, 0224, 0238, 0294, 0424,
0668, 0671, 0775, 0792, 0951,
0962, 0993

Shannita Williams-Alleyne, Craftydiva Designs, USA
Swalleyne@pacbell.net
0068, 0649

Brittany Wilson, Bohemian Knitter Chic, USA
Bohoknitterchic@yahoo.com
bohoknitterchic.etsy.com
0131, 0226, 0280, 0307, 0326,
0336, 0457, 0464, 0621, 0624,
0743

Julie Witt, Canada
juliewitt@shaw.ca
sewknitful.blogspot.com
0267, 0947

Jacqueline Wolk, USA
jacqueline_wolk@yahoo.com
hellojackie.blogspot.com
0315, 0351, 0363, 0375

Essie Woods Bruell, Turtlefat Collection, USA
ewoodsb@aol.com
www.turtlefat.com
0095, 0112, 0247, 0306, 0346,
0371, 0379, 0462, 0469, 0852,
0943

Woolly Wormhead, UK
mail@woollywormhead.com
www.woollywormhead.com
0008, 0020, 0021, 0022, 0043,
0049, 0050, 0051, 0052, 0054,
0142, 0157, 0158, 0176, 0177,
0215, 0229, 0253, 0318, 0447,
0450, 0578, 0603, 0627, 0800,
0802, 0803, 0811, 0818, 0831,
0833, 0839, 0858, 0909, 0929,
0937

Patricia Would, Cottonon, UK
sandp.would@tiscali.co.uk
0019, 0041, 0042, 0056, 0190,
0232, 0273, 0571, 0595, 0599,
0609, 0617, 0626, 0633, 0646,
0733, 0736, 0776, 0785, 0972

About the Author

Annie Modesitt is a hand-knit designer, writer, and teacher based in St. Paul, Minnesota. After a long hiatus from knitting during the 1990s, while she earned her master's in costume and set design from Rutgers University and worked for the weekly *Martha Stewart Living* television show, she returned to a life of crafting after the birth of her two children. A member of United Scenic Artists, she has worked as a milliner and costume assistant on Broadway, thus developing her love of hats and headpieces.

Modesitt has written many books on knitting (or the effect of knitting on one woman's daily life), including *Confessions of a Knitting Heretic, Cheaper Than Therapy, Twist & Loop, Romantic Hand Knits, Men Who Knit and the Dogs Who Love Them*, and *Knit with Courage, Live with Hope.* She has also authored *Knitted Millinery*, a how-to book on creating fine, wired knitted hats. She also created the clever "Flip Knits" series to demonstrate knitting techniques using a handheld animated flip book.

Currently at work on *History on Two Needles*, an exploration of knit design using artwork from various periods as inspiration points, Modesitt divides her time between designing and working at home and traveling around the world teaching unsuspecting knitters how to rethink the way they knit and purl. She lives with her husband, Gerry, two wonderful children, various cats, and Atticus, the wonder-Standard-Poodle.